Never Too Early

Rearing Godly Children Who Love to Learn

— by **Doreen Claggett**

About my mom and this book . . .

If someone were to ask me, "Who is the first person you think of when you need the solid godly counsel of an older woman?" I would respond, every time, without hesitation, "My mother, of course!" She is simply the most beautiful person I have ever known. I often ask my mother after bringing her my most recent problem or confusion over how to handle my very strong-willed two-year-old, "Mom, how do other young women ever survive without someone like you to talk to?" Well, now every woman can benefit from some of the best advice my mom has offered to me about how to love my husband and children God's way. This includes not only principles for everyday living but also the principles and methods for educating my children in Christ beginning in their formative years.

I'm sure this book will be a constant encouragement and resource to you, as my mom is continually to me, ever pointing me back to what she calls her formula for joy: "Put God first, others next (particularly your husband and children), and yourself last."

Lynda Claggett Maxwell

(Lynda is pictured on the cover with her husband, Anthony, and their two children, Victoria and Gabriel.)

Never Too Early

by **Doreen Claggett**

author of the Christ-Centered
Curriculum for Early Childhood program

NEVER TOO EARLY

Claggett Ministries may be contacted through Rocky Bayou Christian School, 2101 N. Partin Drive, Niceville, FL 32578.

Cover design incorporates the logo of Christ Centered Publications, Inc., Niceville, FL. Used by permission.

Cover layout by Jack Duffy, former Marketing and Advertising Consultant for Christ Centered Publications.

Cover photos by Brenda Jordan Photography, Niceville, FL.

Printed in the United States of America

Except where noted, all Scripture quotations in this book are from The Holy Bible, New King James Version, ©1982 by Thomas Nelson, Inc.

❧ DEDICATION ❧

This book is lovingly dedicated to my best friend and husband of 35 years, Herbert Edward Claggett, and our four wonderful children and their spouses — Joseph and Denise Claggett, Randall and Linda Claggett, Shari and Mark Turner, and Lynda and Tony Maxwell — in whom we find great delight as we see them "passing on the faith" to our precious grandchildren: Amanda, Jennifer, and Ashley Claggett, Shannon Claggett, Michael and Lauren Turner (twins), and Victoria and Gabriel Maxwell.

To God Almighty be the honor and glory for any fruit from this labor of love, for it is "of him, and through him, and to him . . . to whom be glory forever. Amen." (Rom 11:36)

TABLE OF CONTENTS

⚹ Reference Material ⚹

Appreciation is extended to the following authors and publishers who allowed me to quote their material herein.

Bloom, Allan, *The Closing of the American Mind*. Copyright ©1983 by Allan Bloom. All rights reserved. Published by Simon and Schuster, New York. Used by permission.

Blumenfeld, Samuel, *Who Killed Excellence?* Copyright ©1985 by Samuel Blumenfeld. All rights reserved. Published in *Imprimis* magazine, Vol. 14, No. 9. Used by permission.

Brownfield, Allan C., *Why Are Our Schools Producing Illiterates?* Copyright ©1981 by Allan C. Brownfield. All rights reserved. Published in *Human Events* newspaper, August 17, 1985. Used by permission.

Chall, Jeanne S., *Learning To Read: The Great Debate*. Copyright ©1981 by Jeanne S. Chall. All rights reserved. Published by McGraw-Hill, New York. Used by permission.

Coalition of Revival, Inc. *The Christian World View of Science and Technology*. Copyright ©1986 by The Coalition of Revival, Inc. All rights reserved. Published by The Coalition of Revival, Inc., Mountain View, California. Used by permission.

Cohen, A., *Everyman's Talmud*. Copyright ©1949 by A. Cohen. All rights reserved. Published by E. P. Dutton Co., New York. Used by permission.

Cowman, Mrs. Charles E., *Streams in the Desert*. Copyright ©1950 by Mrs. Charles E. Cowman. All rights reserved. Published by Cowman Publications, Inc., Los Angeles, California. Used by permission.

Earle, Alice Morse. *Child Life in Colonial Days*. Copyright ©1899 by Alice Morse Earle. All rights reserved. Published by the MacMillan Co. Used by permission.

Elkind, David. *The Hurried Child*. Copyright ©1985 by David Elkind. All rights reserved. Published by Addison-Wesley Publishing Company, New York. Used by permission.

Ezzo, Gary and Anne Marie, *Preparation for Parenting*. Copyright ©1986 by Gary and Anne Marie Ezzo. All rights reserved. Published by Grace Community Church, Sun Valley, California. Used by permission.

McCurry, Robert, *Parents and the Education of Their Children.* Copyright ©1985 by Robert McCurry. All rights reserved. Published by Temple Press, East Point, Georgia. Used by permission.

Peter, Dr. Lawrence J., *Peter's Quotations: Ideas For Our Time.* Copyright ©1977 by Dr. Lawrence J. Peter. All rights reserved. Published by Bantam Books, New York. Used by permission.

Phillips, Phil, *Turmoil in the Toy Box.* Copyright ©1986 by Phil Phillips. All rights reserved. Published by Starburst Publishers, Lancaster, Pennsylvania. Used by permission.

Postman, Neil, *Amusing Ourselves to Death.* Copyright ©1985 by Neil Postman. All rights reserved. Published by Penguin Books, New York. Used by permission.

Schaeffer, Francis A., *Art and the Bible.* Copyright ©1973 by Francis A. Schaeffer. All rights reserved. Published by Inter-Varsity Press, Downers Grove, Illinois. Used by permission.

Schlafly, Phyllis, *The Phyllis Schlafly Report,* Vol. 22, No.1, August 1988. Copyright ©1988 by Phyllis Schlafly. All rights reserved. Used by permission.

Seidel, Leonard J., *God's New Song: A Biblical Perspective of Music.* Copyright ©1973 by Leonard J. Seidel. All rights reserved. Published by Grace Unlimited Publications, Springfield, Virginia. Used by permission.

Sprague, William B., *Annals of the American Pulpit,* Vol.1. Copyright ©1985 by William B. Sprague. All rights reserved. Published by Arnos Press & *The New York Times,* New York. Used by permission.

Stormer, John A., *Growing Up God's Way.* Copyright ©1983 by John A. Stormer. All rights reserved. Published by Liberty Bell Press, Florissant, Missouri. Used by permission.

Taylor, Hudson, *Union and Communion.* Copyright © by J. Hudson Taylor. All rights reserved. Published by Bethany House Publishers, Minneapolis, Minnesota. Used by permission.

Tozer, A.W., *The Knowledge of the Holy.* Copyright ©1961 by A.W. Tozer. All rights reserved. Published by Harper & Row Publishers, San Francisco, California. Used by permission.

Van Der Kooy, T., *Distinctive Features of a Christian School.* Copyright ©1977 by T. Van Der Kooy. All rights reserved. Published in *The Journal of Christian Reconstruction,* Vol. IV, Summer 1977, Vallecito, California. Used by permission.

Weiner, Rose, *Friends of God.* Copyright ©1983 by Rose Weiner. All rights reserved. Published by Maranatha Publications, Gainesville, Florida. Used by permission.

⇸ FOREWORD ⇷

Over the years, I have observed Doreen Claggett's dedication to serve others — and how she actually lives her life daily on the basis of what she understands God would have her to do. This was seen through her teaching of her own kindergarten students, many other teachers through nationwide seminars, and many home schooling parents through her Christ-Centered Curriculum for Early Childhood program. Claggett's tireless dedication to minister to others has often taken a toll on her health, but she recognized that as an attack from Satan to block the teaching of God's Word and continued her work.

One of the major emphases of this book is Early Childhood Education. Mrs. Claggett presents the historical evidence for ECE from the Hebrew culture to Colonial America. It was during this special time in our country's history when many of our greatest leaders were trained up by their parents. She also has experienced proven results of ECE from 21 years of teaching three-, four-, five-, and six-year-olds who have flourished under her approach and the materials she developed. I don't know about the reader, but as for me I'll take history and tangible results over theory and academia every time. This book challenges the widely accepted delayed-education theory with the best of all rebuttals — truth. The proponents of delayed education may attempt to discredit her, but they won't be able to repudiate the truth she presents.

J. Richard Fugate,

Author, *What the Bible Says . . . About Child Training,*
Successful Home Schooling, Will Early Education RUIN Your Child?

❧ Preface ❦

It was a chilly November evening, in 1979. The brilliant fire, which had once so crisply crackled in the fireplace, was now only a pleasant soft glow of burning embers. Sitting on the edge of the raised brick hearth, basking in the radiant beauty and warmth of the now still fire, I was deep in thought. Bob Grete, Director of Rocky Bayou Christian School (RBCS) in Niceville, Florida, had just finished his weekly staff Bible study. When he sat down nearby, I finally mustered the courage to ask what had been on my heart for a long time: "Do you think I have any potential to write professionally?"

For some time, as RBCS Kindergarten Director, I'd already been corresponding with Bob in daily notes which shared exciting new things God was revealing about early childhood education. Before testing the "discoveries" out on him, I reworded, again and again, wanting the communication to be "just right." In those days, his responses came back with brief, encouraging comments on my questions, plus plenty of red marks as "corrections."

As I awaited his reply, it seemed as if the world had suddenly stopped. Thoughts then ran rampant in my mind: "What will he say? If he says, 'No,' how does that fit with my ever-increasing 'drive' to put what I'm learning on paper? But then," I argued with myself, "who am I to even consider such a thing as writing professionally?"

Then, through Bob, came what proved to be my heavenly Father's life-changing answer. Nothing profound; just a simple, "Yes, you do." Not long afterward, the Lord began to show that what I called a "drive" was actually His working in me "both to will and do for His good pleasure (Phil 2:13)." As each year passed, experience in writing increased, as did my understanding of the biblical perspective of early childhood.

Though I feel no more "qualified" today than I did then, I've learned to consistently abide in Christ, as my Vine. For I now know experientially that apart from Him I really can't do anything of eternal value (John 15:5)! But with God, all things are possible (Mark 10:27)! And that is the way it should be.

Therefore, in spite of an at-times "overwhelming" sense of my own inadequacies, I've sought to obey the Lord by writing this book. I don't come to you with a long list of "the world's credentials." I can only come to you with a devoted heart who simply responded: "When You said, 'Seek My face,' my heart said to You, 'Your face, LORD, I will seek (Psa 27:8).'" This book is a result of that hungering and thirsting after His face! From the depth of my being, it is my unceasing prayer that God clearly communicate His heart to you — and nothing of "Doreen."

As an older woman, I'm writing especially to younger women, that you may learn how to biblically love your husbands and your children (Titus 2:4). That does not mean, however, that husbands can't find profit in the book. On the contrary, husbands should read it. As your wife's teacher and protector, you are responsible for discerning whether she is being taught according to God's truth.

Christian school administrators and kindergarten teachers will also find profit in this book. As the Director of a kindergarten following this philosophy, I've witnessed God's rich blessings upon its implementation. In addition, as a Kindergarten Director, I would make every effort to get a copy into the hands of each student's mom.

"Now to Him who is able to do exceedingly abundantly above all that we ask or think, according to the power that works in us, to Him be glory in the church by Christ Jesus to all generations, forever and ever. Amen (Eph 3:20-21)."

Doreen Claggett

❧ ACKNOWLEDGMENTS ❧

Heartfelt appreciation goes to my mentor of 21 years, Bob Grete, Superintendent of Rocky Bayou Christian School (RBCS) in Niceville, Florida. His continual godly counsel and encouragement to pursue the biblical study of early childhood education has meant more than words can express. I'm also grateful to others associated with RBCS who contributed biblical insights on mathematics (Michael Mosley and Carla Alldredge), history (Cathy-Anna Faile and Ned Brande), science (Brian Alldredge), art (Ron Dougherty), and music (Bill Cain).

Extra special thanks go to my friend, J. Richard Fugate, author of *What the Bible Says . . . About Child Training*, for encouraging me to write this book and for backing up the encouragement by investing his time reviewing the manuscript plus offering numerous helpful comments. Ron Brackin was a Godsend during a critical time in the manuscript's final preparation! His gracious editorial assistance made it possible to meet publishing deadlines. Gregg Harris, author of *The Christian Home School* and Director of Christian Life Workshops, also provided helpful insights. Maynard Hatcher, a student of ancient near Eastern literature and history for more than 35 years, was gracious enough to provide resource materials and suggestions which greatly aided writing on Hebrew education.

My husband Ed's belief that the Lord has given something truly worth sharing and that I really could write this book helped me to persevere. As a "writer's widower" for numerous years, he has generously sacrificed both time and money to make possible writing on principles of being a godly wife and mother who educates her young children biblically. Ed has been both a wonderful husband and father, for which I praise God continually!

Introduction

CATCHING THE VISION:

God-Centered Early Education

"If the foundations are destroyed, What can the righteous do? [For] where there is no vision, the people perish . . ." (Psa 11:3; Prov 29:18).

When I was a little girl, it may have looked like I was just playing with dolls, but really, I was privately dreaming of the day I would become a real mom — just like my mommy.

She was such a joyous example! I wanted to be just like her. I was much older before it even occurred to me that I might want to be like anybody else.

Even as a preschooler, I couldn't wait until I could run a household, be a wife, and, of course, rear my own children. Why? Because my mother had made such a positive impact on my heart, my mind, my very spirit — everything that makes me who I am today!

So, mothers, never doubt the immense difference you can make in your children's lives. The hand that rocks the cradle indeed is the hand that rules the world.

Yes!

By your example and your every word, *you* are shaping tomorrow.

WHEN YOU TEACH that two-year-old that he must not hit back, you are teaching a future daddy — and possible future world leader or missionary or nuclear physicist — that vengeance is not the proper response to evil.

When you cradle that weeping three-year-old in your arms, you demonstrate — far more than any words can attempt to teach — the joy of bearing one another's hurts and the sharing nature of real love. You are embedding in the heart and mind of a future parent and/or corporate manager and/or astronaut and/or mighty evangelist the beautiful experience of godly compassion, sensitivity, empathy, and heart-felt sympathy.

And when you enthusiastically praise and hug your 18-month-old for uttering the word "please," you are building an important base: showing the toddler that effort is its own reward, that striving toward a challenge is wonderful, and indeed: that learning is a joy!

Rearing godly children who love to learn is such a precious responsibility for today's mother! As you seek the Lord and wait on His guidance, you'll find that your Creator has, indeed, equipped you to be a godly role model.

Your nurturing, compassionate example is so important during those formative years from birth to age 6. During that vital time, most of your child's personality, character, habits, and intellectual makeup is established.

But just being a good example is only the start! You also are your child's first teacher. So much of the way adults deal with life is learned right there at their mother's knee.

I challenge you to prepare yourself for this vital role — to learn how to educate your child biblically. You can be ready right from the very start. From your child's earliest days, you can instill in your child a God-centered perspective of life.

I believe, in these increasingly turbulent days, we moms must.

For that child in your arms may be the next Billy Graham.

Or Madame Curie.

Or George Washington.

Or Florence Nightingale.

AFTER OUR WEDDING, my wonderful husband Ed and I waited four long but memorable years before we finally held our firstborn in our arms. Joey's arrival brought us such great joy! From the moment I first cuddled him in my arms, my gratitude to God overflowed in feelings too great to put into words.

The Lord wisely spaced the next three children two years apart each — and as Randy, Shari, and Lynda were born, my gratitude for God's gift grew.

Somehow, I had not heard the debate in academic circles over whether to teach — or not to teach — during their formative years. Thus, doing what came naturally, I simply taught constantly. First, and foremost, I taught them about the Lord — even before they could speak! Talking to them (no baby talk), and then with them, was the norm. It seemed as natural as breathing! I taught letters, sounds, and numbers. Our family spent marvelous times together discovering and enjoying God's world.

All of our children learned to read early. They remained several years above their grade levels throughout their school years. Three graduated as Most Outstanding Student. All consistently achieved honor roll status.

My husband and I have always sought to develop each son and daughter according to individual God-given capabilities.

Looking back, I recall feeling no pressure. Nor do the children. They remember only excitement over each new thing they were learning. Those were wonderful years! When our youngest, Lynda, was three-and-a-half, God opened a door which continued to utilize my deep longing to mother. In

1973, I was given the opportunity to work with the kindergartners at Rocky Bayou Christian School in Niceville, Florida.

Even though RBCS had no three-year-old program at
the time, I agreed to accept if Lynda could be with me. She
joined the others and did beautifully! The key to effective
teaching proved very simple: "Lord, You created these little
ones. Please show me what they can handle. What do You want
for them?" As the years progressed, the Lord put pressure on me
— pressure to keep up with their delight in learning!

NOT UNTIL THE EARLY '80s did I become aware of the
early childhood debate in academic realms. As I understand it, the controversy deals with at what age a child should
begin to be taught academically, especially how to read, and
with what intensity. At one extreme is the "Super Baby" approach with its push-push emphasis from infancy. At the other
is the *laissez-faire* emphasis on fun, learn-when-he-decides-for-
himself view. Since, for many years, RBCS kindergartners had
enjoyed learning while achieving high academic results, it
appeared that what was happening in our classrooms fit somewhere in the middle.

However, after learning about those and other view-
points, I felt led to more intensively pursue a biblical view on
early childhood education. That launched an extended period
of studying. An outcome of that was the development of the
"Christ-Centered Curriculum for Early Childhood" program
(published by Christ Centered Publications, located on the
campus of Rocky Bayou Christian School), plus biblical early
childhood seminars.

During my seminar travels, I've had the privilege of talking with numerous young parents and Christian school kindergarten teachers. Repeatedly, moms have expressed an
instinctive feeling that their preschoolers are ready to learn.
"But then," both moms and teachers would question, "what

about all those warnings of the dangers from teaching too early?" In reaction to the warnings, some report using an entertainment approach to make learning "fun, fun, fun." However, the type of character being evidenced in these children as they get older is causing concern. (General lack of interest in learning is one standard complaint.) Still others seek answers on how to deal with negative results from having pushed preschoolers too much.

FROM THOSE TALKS, it's evident that more and more are searching for a biblical alternative to the two extremes — "Super Babies" vs. "let them wait." At one time or another, most have felt this basic confusion: "If our nation's leading child psychologists and educators can't agree on what's 'best,' how are we going to discern the truth?" God isn't the author of such confusion (1 Cor 14:33). He holds the answers: "If any of you lacks wisdom, let him ask of God, who gives to all liberally and without reproach, and it will be given to him" (James 1:5).

This book is an end product of taking God at His Word in James 1:5. I make no claim to have found all of Christ's answers. But I do believe that the biblical truths I've learned thus far are worth sharing. My approach is not to discuss in depth the views of force-feeding academics to children too young, or holding them back. Rather, I'll be focusing on what I'm convinced is the traditional Bible-believing parental position on early childhood education.

That traditional Bible-believing position involves restoring God to His rightful place on the throne in parents' lives first. Why is that so necessary? Before little ones ever learn to read, they'll first "read" the lives of parents, because believers are Christ's "letters," known and read of all men (2 Cor 3:2-3). What they "read" affects their concept of God, thus their spiritual, moral, and academic development. Parenting is a precious yet serious privilege.

CONSIDER GOD'S LESSON PLAN for how parents are to educate His heritage:

> Sh'ma Yisrael, Adonai Elohenu, Adonai Echad.
> Baruch Shem, K'vod Malchuto Le Olam Va Ed.

> **Hear, O Israel: The Lord our God, the Lord is One. Praised be His Name, whose glorious kingdom is forever and ever.**

With these words, the Jewish people declare their ownership at the beginning of each shabbat, or sabbath. And, with these words, Moses proclaimed God's will to His sons and daughters and to their sons and daughters.

> *"You shall love the* LORD *your God with all your heart, with all your soul, and with all your strength.*

> *"And these words which I command you today shall be in your heart.*

> *"You shall teach them diligently to your children, and shall talk of them when you sit in your house, when you walk by the way, when you lie down, and when you rise up" (Deut 6:5-7).*

BLESSINGS FOR OBEDIENCE

Jesse obeyed God. Listen to the testimony of his son, David:

> *"Oh, how I love Your law! It is my meditation all the day. You, through Your commandments, make me wiser than my enemies; For they are ever with me. I have more understanding than all my teachers, For Your testimonies are my meditation. I understand more than the ancients, Because I keep Your precepts. I have restrained my feet from every evil way, That I may Keep Your word. I have not departed from Your judgments, For You Yourself have taught me. How sweet are Your words to my taste, Sweeter than honey to my mouth! Through Your*

precepts I get understanding; Therefore I hate every
false way"(Psa 119:97-104).

Jesse knew God's law, the Torah. He not only heard God's Word, he obeyed it. Jesse was a disciple. And he passed that knowledge and love on to David. He discipled David. And, as a disciple of God, David, too, loved God and His law. He declared to everyone that God's law made him wiser than his enemies, gave him more insight than all his teachers and more understanding than the elders.

God, David said, personally revealed Himself to him through His Word. And that knowledge was sweeter than honey.

PROVIDING A CHRISTIAN EDUCATION

Jesse and David painted a vivid picture of the process of Christian education. Peter later summarized it as "giving all diligence, add to your faith virtue, to virtue knowledge ..." (2 Pet 1:5).

First, we become disciples of God. Then we actively, constantly, and purposefully teach our children the love, discipline, and understanding of God's Word.

Using God's pattern, then, we can define Christian education as:

the process of God working through committed teachers using biblical methods and truthful curriculum materials to bring forth disciples who hold the biblical world view and possess the godly character and academic skills necessary to fulfill God's calling and live for His glory.

Faith, virtue, knowledge — for the mother first, then for the child. In practice, however, Christian education is an ongoing process, rather like sanctification. The Holy Spirit continues to disciple us as we disciple our children.

THE WORM IN THE APPLE

As with everything else in God's kingdom, the devil wastes no time manufacturing a counterfeit in the hope of cheating God's children out of their inheritance. Public education has become such a counterfeit.

First, the devil slashed into **God's Cycle of Education** with the **Dagger of Secularization** and replaced **Faith in God** with **Faith in Man** (the religion of Secular Humanism).

Finding no opposition to that procedure, he returned and removed Virtue, replacing it with Situation Ethics and Values Clarification.

This operation effectively left Knowledge man-centered and relative, instead of God-centered and absolute.

In the meantime, a similar metamorphosis was taking place in the Christian schools. But here, the devil was a little more subtle.

INSTEAD OF USING SECULAR HUMANISM and Situation Ethics to replace Faith and Virtue, he introduced the notion of "sacred versus secular." Bible, he said, is sacred: history, language, reading, math, and science are secular, or neutral. The implication: God belongs in the Bible; He does not belong in the world. This was fine with the devil. He had no objection at all to God being "tacked on" to Christian education.

Some schools saw through the deception and determined to "integrate" God into all academic subjects. But the attempt did little more than throw "Bible darts" at them, and the end result was still more humanistic than godly.

RESTORING EDEN

But we can recapture God's original plan in which Christ is the center, the focal point of the teacher, the methods, and the curriculum if we learn to teach every discipline from its rudiments and principles in Scripture. God did not intend His Word to be added to man's. It is to be the *foundation*, the standard, the objective truth that is taught to our children. It all begins with you and with me and our personal relationship to Jesus.

Part I: Becoming a Disciple

Chapter One
Becoming Nurtured in God's Word

"You shall love the Lord your God with all your heart, with all your soul, and with all your strength. And these words which I command you today shall be in your heart. You shall teach them diligently to your children, and shall talk of them when you sit in your house, when you walk by the way, when you lie down, and when you rise up" (Deut 6:5-7).

First, "you shall love." Then, "you shall teach."

Loving God with our whole being is life's most satisfying goal! This is a discipling process by which God's children learn to "hear" and "do" all that He has commanded. It begins with a submissive spirit, asking God to produce that fruit in us. Then, as He teaches us, we are to pass that faith on to our children.

Discipling is a specific type of training which nurtures in God's Word and His ways. God disciples us so we can disciple those He entrusts to us.

Unless we love Jesus supremely, above all others, He tells us that we can't even be His disciples (Luke 14:26).

Loving God supremely means that we esteem nothing of more worth to us than He is. As a result, we willingly put our "self" life on the cross daily. To be His disciples (pupils or learners), a submissive spirit is essential (Luke 14:27, 33). For teachable hearts are the foundation of fruitful learning — at any age.

Loving God that supremely is the fruit of being discipled (taught) by the living Word, Jesus Christ, through His written Word.

Being nurtured in His Truth is what sets us free from self to love Him as we ought (John 8:31–32). Christ's love is the power Source to love others sacrificially, as He has loved us. A commitment to love in this manner testifies that we are His disciples (John 13:34–35). All relationships in life center around these two loves (Matt 22:37–40).

Every day represents an individualized, God-designed lesson plan to demonstrate such love as an act of worship. In other words, we should show His "worthship" by how we live. By God's power, choosing to do things His way instead of our own is the essence of true worship.

Worship isn't something reserved for Sundays or quiet times with the Lord. All of life is meant to be an act of worship, as His living sacrifices (Rom 12:1–2). In so losing our lives for Christ's sake, we will find them (Matt 16:25). That style of living will bear much fruit, thus glorifying God. So shall we become His disciples (John 15:8).

Having a worshiping submission to God is thus the first step toward biblically loving our husbands and children — our highest calling in life.

None of us are able, on our own, to fulfill this blessed calling (John 15:5). Beloved, God isn't after ability, but availability. Being willing for God to do whatever it takes to produce such fruit is our responsibility; working it out in us is His.

If you're like I was, you want to make that commitment, but you're afraid. In my case, I had a misunderstanding of just who God is and how He works in us. For example, I used to think that if I committed my life to God He'd remove everyone and everything I loved in order to have first place. Because I loved my husband Ed more than God, I was afraid He'd take him away from me.

At that time, I knew Ed better than God. I didn't under-stand God's marvelous "worthship" because my conception of Him was wrong. To me, the God of the Old Testament was harsh and judgmental, like my own father at times, even though he loved me. (In the eyes of a child, a parent stands in place of God Himself.) Yet, the God of the New Testament was the gen-tle, loving Jesus. I feared the OT image but felt desperately drawn to the NT one. Release from that fear came only through learning that the God of the Old Testament is Jesus Christ! How important that our concept of God be biblical. A. W. Tozer wrote:

> . . . *Having a right conception of God is basic not only to systematic theology but to practical Christian living as well. It is to worship what the foundation is to the temple; where it is inadequate or out of plumb the whole structure must sooner or later collapse.*[1]

So then, acquiring an accurate understanding of God is foundational to becoming His disciple. The Holy Scriptures are His means for doing so. In them He reveals His true worth. He unfolds His personality, preferences, and passions, and His experi-ences, expectations, and the extent of His faithfulness and mercy.

When we freely commit our lives to God, we will dis-cover as China missionary Dr. J. Hudson Taylor discovered: "A wondrously glad surprise. No Moriah, no Calvary; on the con-trary, a King! When the heart submits, then Jesus reigns. And when Jesus reigns, there is rest."[2]

In the rest of such submission, Jesus ever so lovingly teaches what we need to know about being His disciples. He nurtures through His Word in five fundamental areas: hearing, reading, studying, memorizing and meditating. All five are nec-essary to grow in the faith as He intends.

If all we do is hear the Word preached, we're like a per-son trying to grasp a softball with just our little finger. Adding hearing plus faithful reading is better, and adding study is better still. But we cannot get much of a hold on the ball with only three fingers. We need all four fingers and an opposing thumb to firmly grasp a softball, and we need to hear, read, study, memorize, and meditate upon God's Word in order to firmly grasp the Scriptures. Thus, when the storms of life assail, our life's foundation is secure because it's grounded in the Rock (Matt 7:24-25)!

HEARING THE WORD

We know that "faith comes by hearing, and hearing by the word of God" (Rom 10:17). This is true for both saving and sanctifying faith (John 17:17). Sanctifying faith is a purification process; it is the "doing" part of spiritual growth. Christ has ordained the local church to be His main channel for both hearing and doing His Word.

Hearing the preaching of the Word builds love for God. Corporate praise, giving thanks through congregational singing, prayer, and cheerful giving are proper responses to that love (Heb 13:15, 2 Cor 9:7). They are acts of worship which bring great joy to His heart.

Loving God's family also brings Him great pleasure. This fulfills His second great command: "You shall love your neighbor as yourself" (Matt 22:38). In other words, we are to be as sensitive to meet others' needs as we are our own. Faithfully acting in the best interest of others, regardless of how we may "feel" personally about them, is the highest form of loving.

For instance, it is in the best interest of our brethren to love them without hypocrisy. It is in their best interest for us to hate evil and cling to good, to show affection, considering others better than ourselves, and to diligently serve them by exercising our spiritual gift(s) in the body. (See Romans 12:6-8 and 1 Corinthians 12.) They are blessed when we set an example of rejoicing in hope and being patient in tribulation. They are victorious when we steadfastly continue in prayer on their be-half. Love distributes to the needs of the saints and is given to showing hospitality. We love by blessing those who persecute us and returning good for evil. Love rejoices with those who re-joice and weeps with those who weep. We demonstrate our love when we live peaceably with our brothers and sisters. Love does not avenge when wronged. In short, applied biblical love means not being overcome by evil but overcoming evil with good. (See Romans 12:9-21.)

Not only should His love be applied toward the house-hold of faith but also toward unbelievers. It is the same as doing it for Christ when we invite the lost into our homes for a meal, to spend the night or meet their physical needs (Matt 25:40). Taking the initiative to make a friend is often the key which opens his or her heart to receiving the Word. Some have to see faith in action in order to believe it. Therefore, we should pray for both opportunity and timing to share the gospel. We can trust the Lord for fruit in His own time. We plant, another wa-ters, but it is God who gives the increase (1 Cor 3:7). Impor-tunate praying (keeping on keeping on) for the salvation of others is wise (Prov 11:30).

The role model we set in the local ministry also impacts the way our children will function in the Body of Christ. This is especially true when it comes to how we handle troubled waters in the family of God. Children need to see Christ's love demonstrated during times of church squabbles, murmuring and complaining, leadership falling into sin, or a church split. How these sins are handled not only sets a pattern for our chil-dren's future church relationships but also affects relationships in our own families.

Commitment means working out, not bailing out. There are no perfect homes; thus there are no perfect churches. (Sepa-ration from a local body should come about only after much prayer and the clear leading of the Holy Spirit.) Faithfully gathering together to hear and do God's Word is still His perfect plan. It is part of being a living sacrifice, holy and acceptable to God.

READING THE WORD

Untended fires soon go out. So it is with the fire of our love for God. This needs regular refueling to maintain its strength. For that reason, we should pray for hearts that sing: "I will delight myself in Your statutes; I will not forget Your word" (Psa 119:16).

Reading the Scriptures should be done with a clean conscience, having confessed known sins so He can hear our prayers for enlightenment. Unconfessed sin blocks our lines of communication (Psa 66:18). When we confess by agreeing with God that a thought or action is sin, we receive forgiveness and cleansing (John 1:9). Once the lines of communication are open, we can pray: "Open my eyes, that I may see Wondrous things from Your law" (Psa 119:18).

At the very least, the entire Bible should be read completely through once a year. This can be done by reading three or four chapters each day or almost 23 chapters per week. Many Bibles include a daily reading schedule. The best I have found is *The One Year Bible* (Wheaton, IL: Tyndale House Publishers, Inc., 1986). The Bible is divided into 365 dated readings. Each day, in sequence, a passage is read from the Old Testament, New Testament, Psalms, and Proverbs.

It is best if Bible reading can be done at a set time each day, especially before our families arise. We need to allow time for talking with the Lord and giving Him sufficient, uninterrupted time to talk to us. Personal worship, praise, and prayer prevents our quiet time from becoming mechanical. We should talk to the King in His language by praising, worshiping, and praying from Scripture. (Until large portions of Scripture are memorized, this can be done with an open Bible in front of you and changing the words slightly to make it more personal. A great place to start is with the Psalms!)

Watch out for Satan's distraction darts (1 Pet 5:8)! He knows just what it will take to turn our heads. Psalm 119 is a great defense. Over and over it extols the excellencies of God's Word and the fruit its reading can bring in our lives.

STUDYING THE WORD

As our love for God's Word increases through reading it, the Holy Spirit prompts us to even deeper exploration. Studying God's Word yields greater fruit and requires greater self-discipline. However, this is all part of becoming a faithful disciple. Reading covers general concepts; studying provides deeper insights into particular areas of study.

As we study, we shouldn't expect man to be as God. Notes in study Bibles, commentaries, and other study aids should be approached as a good Berean. In other words, we should hear the Word with all readiness of mind (a teachable heart) but search the Scriptures to make sure we are receiving Truth (Acts 17:11).

A commentary, such as J. Sidlow Baxter's *Explore the Book*, read concurrently with Bible readings can be beneficial. It is also helpful to look for particular themes. To establish the proper fear or reverence for the Lord, I recommend beginning with the theme of God's sovereignty. For example, this morning I read 1 Chronicles 12:19-14:17; Romans 1:1-17; and Psalm 9:13-20. In those passages, I learned that "David's fame spread throughout every land, and the LORD made all the nations fear him (NIV)." In Romans 1:10, Paul revealed God's sovereignty when he prayed: "by God's will the way may be opened for me to come to you (NIV)."

Marking such passages, perhaps with colored felt pens or highlighters, will fill your Bible with samples of Jesus as Lord of lords and King of kings. A real faith builder! Since all the commandments hinge on two, it also helps to mark all instructions related to how we are to love God and others. Use a different color for each topic.

Along with daily readings, it is helpful to use a weekly schedule designed to study a particular book in-depth, specific areas of doctrine, or biblical principles. Evening study periods once or twice a week can be added to study a book in-depth using more detailed individual commentaries. Additional studies could focus on specific subjects using aids to doctrinal studies.

An especially helpful book is *Explore the Word!* by Henry M. Morris, III. (Available through Master Books, P. O. Box 1602, El Cajon, CA 92022.) This resource tool shows how to study the Bible using *Strong's Exhaustive Concordance.* The book begins with instructions for the novice then gradually intensifies the depth of study. Thus, it can be an ongoing valuable resource for continual growth!

In order to "rightly divide the word of truth," be sure to study all passages within their biblical context. Read the passages before and after the passage in question, note the historical setting (differences in cultures can affect meanings), asking the Holy Spirit: "What does this mean? And that? Why did You put that there?" Search diligently for His answers, and ask Him to guide you to truth (John 16:13).

A Bible study program of this nature, integrated with earnest prayer along with church and Bible studies, will increase your love and faith in Christ. Adding memorization and meditation to such study puts you that much closer to truly delighting in God and lifelong learning.

MEMORIZING THE WORD

"How can a young man cleanse his way? By taking heed according to Your word. . . . Your word I have hidden in my heart, That I might not sin against You" (Psa 119:9-11).

The more the Word is in us, the more the Holy Spirit is able to bring to mind when we are tempted to do things our way instead of God's.

For example, memorizing Psalm 119 (a section at a time) establishes the importance of having God's Word in our minds. Memorizing 1 Corinthians 13 provides practical examples of God's law of love. Ephesians 6:10-18 is an exhortation to put on the whole armor of God so that we don't try living in the energies of the flesh. The Sermon on the Mount (Matthew 5-7) gives practical principles in Christian living. Philippians 4 helps us learn to be content, to watch over our thought life, and to trust God for strength to obey and provision for all our needs.

MEDITATING UPON THE WORD

"Make me understand the way of Your precepts;
So shall I meditate on Your wonderful works" (Psa
119:27).

To meditate implies "chewing" on the Word. A good technique is to "chew" on what we have memorized by mulling it over while driving, washing dishes, making beds, or trying to sleep. A free mind is always an opportunity to grow for Christ. When my mind is unoccupied by my task, I can day-dream, fret, or surrender it to my Lord, who is faithful to then take His Word and make it practical in my life.

Without meditation, we can become forgetful hearers and thus neglectful doers. Scriptural meditation is the root of godly character, because what we meditate upon, we will be-come (Prov 23:7). "Chewing" on God's Word leads to joy (Psa 63:5-6), wisdom (Psa 119:97-100), prosperity (Psa 1:2-3), and success in all we do (1 Tim 4:15). Joshua presented the Israelites with God's plan for being a victorious disciple:

"This Book of the Law shall not depart from your
mouth, but you shall meditate [ponder or study in
pleasure] in it day and night, that you may observe to

do according to all that is written in it. For then you
will make your way prosperous [profitable], and then
you will have good success [intelligence]" (Josh 1:8).

Once nurtured in God's Word, our faithful, loving Lord arranges circumstances to test our knowledge, understanding, and willingness to obey.

To further illustrate how all this works practically, I believe it would be profitable to share a few such lessons from my own life. Most of you will probably find parallels for yours, if not for now, then for the future.

I remained a babe in Christ far too long and had a lot of catching up to do. When God knew I was ready, He enrolled me in Tribulation 101 at good old L. and M. U. (Lord and Master University). For timid souls like me, the very thought of tribulation was frightening. Yet, God says, "In the world you will have tribulation; but be of good cheer, I have overcome the world" (John 16:33b). The Greek word translated "tribulation" has the sense of a "pressing together."

It is interesting that both wheat and grapes must be pressed together to produce bread and wine, symbols of the body and blood of Christ. In much the same way, God presses us from every angle so that we may yield the fruit of the Spirit.

The Greek word translated "tribulation" in John 16:33 is also used in Romans 5:3: ". . . We also glory in tribulations, knowing that tribulation [pressure] produces perseverance; and perseverance, character; and character, hope [unshakable confidence in Jesus Christ]." In other words, pressure is God's lesson plan for all of us. Note that when we experience stresses we are to glory in them. But this is something which has to be learned by experience (Phil 4:11-12).

God used a rapid-fire teaching method to help me to learn contentment. This meant one trial on top of another for a season. During it all, He encouraged me to "Wait on the

Lord; Be of good courage, And He shall strengthen your heart; Wait, I say, on the Lord!" (Psa 27:14). Previously my outlook on endurance was, "Grant me patience, Lord — but hurry!" Now I had to learn to wait, and wait some more until He accomplished His perfect purpose in each lesson.

Lesson I: Will you set your eyes on that which is not?

"For riches certainly make themselves wings;
They fly away like an eagle to heaven" (Prov 23:5).

Going through financial difficulties is an extremely tough lesson. Therefore, it was a tremendous test of faith when suddenly Ed and I were faced with only $300 per month income and a family of six to support. It became even harder when, after many months, in just one day $11,500 we'd been counting on fell through. The freight train of disappointment threatened to derail my faith.

In a desperate state, my husband and I went to a dear friend, Bob Grete, with our "Why?" questioning. In a sympathetic manner, he explained, "I can't tell you why God allowed this. All I know is that just as Joseph couldn't understand why he'd been thrown into a pit, then sold as a slave, and yet he remained faithful, so must you. God worked Joseph's bad situation for good; He'll do the same in yours" (Rom 8:28). The Lord knew that learning to walk by faith, and not by sight, was far more important than answering our prayers as expected (2 Cor 5:7). Even though we lost our home that Christmas and had no money to our name, He provided the best Christmas ever! (Our gracious God later restored another home of our own in a somewhat miraculous fashion.)

Lesson II: God will provide!

"And my God shall supply all your need according to His riches in glory by Christ Jesus"
(Phil 4:13).

During the two years Ed had no salary, God lovingly revealed Himself as Jehovah-Jireh, our Provider. We never went hungry, even though on occasion the timing was close. For example, one summer evening, I said to my family, "Boy, it would sure be neat if we had some hamburger buns to go with these Sloppy Joes!" (By the way, that was the last meat in the house.) Only minutes later, a car pulled up in the driveway. Out climbed a sister from church with a sack of groceries. At the top of the sack was a package of hamburger buns!

Our children never lacked for clothing either. When there was a shortage, without anyone but God knowing the particulars, a sack of clothes was passed on which always contained the necessary articles, in just the right sizes. His abundant answers soon prompted another need: "Mom, we need some hangers for these clothes," son Joey informed me one morning. I suggested that he pray about it. At noon that day, a lady came by RBCS to drop off some newspapers for a paper drive. When I helped her unload them, at the bottom of her car trunk were several bundles of clothes hangers! She then asked, "Do you know anyone who needs some hangers? I was going to throw these away today." What a faith builder for our young son! To me, God is at His greatest when He shows that He cares about even the little things in our lives! Love for Him grew in leaps and bounds during that period.

Lesson III: The Lord makes us righteous.

> "Blessed are those who hunger and thirst for righteousness, For they shall be filled" (Matt 5:6).

As God continually revealed Himself faithful, there was a corresponding enlargement of my faith. Something very special was happening: He was creating an ever-growing hungering

Never Too Early

and thirsting after righteousness. How excited I was when later discovering that this hungering and thirsting was really for Christ because He is our righteousness (1 Cor 1:30)! In other words, righteousness isn't just an aspect of Christian virtue; righteousness is a Person living His life through us (Gal 2:20)! Like the Psalmist, this should cause us to cry out: "As the deer pants for the water brooks, So pants my soul for You, O God, My soul thirsts for God, for the living God" (Psa 42:1-2).

LESSON IV: Study the Word!

> *"Be diligent to present yourself approved unto God, a worker who does not need to be ashamed, rightly dividing the word of truth" (2 Tim 2:15).*

The written Word of God was the key to satisfying my thirst for the living God! But first, He had to further straighten out my thinking. You see, I'd felt that as a woman, studying the Word was beyond me. Therefore, I relied on the gifted teachers in our church. After all, I reasoned, there was spiritual growth simply through listening to them expound the Scriptures. But the Lord knew that hearing about Him "second hand" was only making me think that I knew Him. Therefore, all teaching support was suddenly removed through heartrending circumstances.

During the subsequent two years, there was no real feeding from the pulpit. However, this precious truth gradually took on meaning: "But you have an anointing from the Holy One, and you know all things. But the anointing which you have received from Him abides in you, and you do not need that anyone teach you" (1 John 2:20, 27). How wonderful it was to learn that He is the One who teaches us knowledge (Psa 94:10)! More and more He taught how to search the Scriptures to find answers to many questions (Eph 1:18). God's heart and mine were being further knit together in love.

LESSON V: Prayer works!

". . .Ask, and it will be given you; seek, and you will find; knock, and it will be opened to you" (Luke 11:9).

A deepened love resulted from learning the importance of prayers of importunity. This meant learning to keep on asking, keep on seeking, keep on knocking, until God answered (one way or another). We see an example of this type of praying in Genesis 18:20-32. In that passage, Abraham implored the Lord to spare Sodom and Gomorrah if He found 50 righteous people there. He continued his plea on behalf of 45, 40, and so on, until he stopped with ten. The Lord responded by promising to spare the cities if He found even ten righteous people there. An answer to this type of praying may come quickly, as in Abraham's case, or it can take many, many years. As long as God gives no release to cease petitioning Him, we should continue praying.

In my own life, there were two outstanding examples of this type of praying. The first involved my father's salvation. During the 75-day period my mother was dying in the hospital (three surgeries, gangrene for two months, massive stroke, paralysis), Dad was at home dying of cancer. Because of her extended sufferings, when Mom went to be with the Lord, it was a sweet release. But since Dad wasn't a Christian, his impending death added even greater fervency to the 30 years of prayers already spent. It looked hopeless, because I'd just talked to him about his relationship to God. Dad had become furious and screamed, "You mean to tell me that if I don't believe as you do that I'm going to hell?" Nevertheless, petitioning God for his salvation continued.

Shortly before Dad died, my sister, Ina Rae, presented the gospel once more. At age 77, our strong moral father wept as he acknowledged that he, too, needed Christ as Lord and Savior. Dad was laid to rest just hours before "Father's Day," 1981.

As others honored their dads, Ina Rae and I could smile through our tears, because our precious Savior had made both our parents' funerals triumphant!

The second prayer of importunity was answered quickly. I'd always been impressed with the caliber of faith Jacob displayed when he wrestled with the Lord all night, claiming, "I will not let You go unless You bless me!" (See Genesis 32:22-30.) However, I'd never dared to pray in such a manner. Not until the "Christ-Centered Curriculum for Early Childhood" project was threatened.

At RBCS, we had no massive funding for this project. Over the eight-year period it took to write it and get it to print, it was touch-and-go many a time. A key turning point was the need of a computer, printer, and copy machine capable of enlarging/reducing artwork. An appeal to Bob Grete (RBCS Superintendent) for funding was met with, "I'm so sorry, Doreen, there just isn't any money."

I knew that without those items we could go no farther. Because I believe that teaching children God's Word and ways as they develop academic skills is dear to Him, I could not accept a "No" answer. While driving out of the school parking lot that afternoon, tears flowing profusely, suddenly there was faith to cry: "I will not let You go until You bless me!" In three days, $8,000 arrived to purchase the equipment! He thus made it possible to continue toward bearing much fruit for His sake.

Lesson VI: Keep on, even when you don't feel like it.

"As your days, so shall your strength be"
(Deut 33:25b).

On the heels of losing both Mom and Dad in a short time period, a rare knee "accident" ripped a quarter-size hole down to my kneecap, exposing the bone. (That test was even harder than the botulism which earlier had nearly claimed my life and required a year's recuperation.) Two surgeries, eight months of crutches, and three years of chronic pain gave deeper meaning to keeping on keeping on, even when not feeling like it. "As your days, so shall your strength be" became a moment-by-moment reality!

LESSON VII: God makes sure that all things work together for the good.

". . . He has done all things well . . ."
(Mark 7:37a).

God used that knee injury to produce even more fruit. Though I hadn't felt ready to give up active teaching, the pain made it easier to do so. (Working with little children requires a lot of physical dexterity and endurance.) The Lord was freeing me for His best — providing more teacher training at RBCS, plus time for increased studying and writing.

Developing the curriculum involved being in the Scriptures constantly. Gradually, His Word began to permeate my heart and mind. As this was happening, it was interesting to note a heightened ability to acquire knowledge in areas beyond the Bible itself. Biblical truths began to stand out in historical, philosophical, and technical research. Phonics/reading, history, math, science, art, music, etc., took on new meaning as His nature showed through in these disciplines. The outcome was that my heart and mind had been tutored to delight in Jesus Christ and lifelong learning. This meant having an ever-increasing sense of what He means by loving Him supremely!

LESSON VIII: Persecution will come!

". . . All who desire to live godly in Christ Jesus
will suffer persecution" (2 Tim 3:12).

Delighting in Christ results in facing periodic crucial turning points. This happens to all who mean business for the

Lord. How we respond in each crisis-hour can mean the difference between great strides forward in faith or spiritual stagnancy, aptly described by Mrs. Charles E. Cowman in the book *Streams in the Desert*:

> *There comes a crisis-hour to each of us, if God has called us to the highest and best, when all resources fail; when we face either ruin or something higher than we ever dreamed; when we must have infinite help from God and yet, ere we can have it, we must let something go; we must surrender completely; we must cease from our own wisdom, strength, and righteousness, and become crucified with Christ and alive in Him. God knows how to lead us up to this crisis, and He knows how to lead us through.*[3]

My particular crisis-hour required carrying out biblical convictions at great cost. For example, the completion years of developing the "Christ-Centered Curriculum for Early Childhood" program involved an utter sense of being totally alone. Rarely did anyone understand the "drive" behind its creation (Phil 2:13). Opposition (sometimes fierce) to the program's development was common. Yet, to do otherwise than follow hard after God's highest and best would, to me, have been sin.

Choosing to press on, allowing Him to crucify self through teaching to respond biblically to opposition, was extremely difficult. Many a time, all earthly resources failed. No one but God fully identified with the deep pain from circumstances surrounding the birth of that vision: "I was crushed . . . so much so that I despaired even of life, but that was to make me rely not on myself, but on the God who raises the dead" (2 Cor 1:8, 9). That period could best be described in *Streams in the Desert*:

- *Pressed out of measure and pressed to all length;*
- *Pressed so intensely it seems, beyond strength;*
- *Pressed in the body and pressed in the soul,*

- *Pressed in the mind till the dark surges roll.*
- *Pressure by foes, and a pressure from friends.*
- *Pressure on pressure, till life nearly ends.*
- *Pressed into knowing no helper but God;*
- *Pressed into loving the staff and the rod.*
- *Pressed into liberty where nothing clings;*
- *Pressed into faith for impossible things.*
- *Pressed into living a life in the Lord.*
- *Pressed into living a Christ-life outpoured.*

Being pressed beyond measure until no one but God was left at the helm reveals that "the life that is lived unto God, however it forfeits human companionships, knows Divine fellowship," continues the author. That alone is worth any price!

The world tells us to "look out for Number One!" "You only go around once," it says, "so go for the gusto!"

But Christ tells us,

> *"If anyone desires to come after Me, let him deny himself, and take up his cross, and follow Me. For whoever desires to save his life will lose it, but whoever loses his life for My sake will find it" (Matt 16:24-25).*

Christ came that we might live life more abundantly (John 10:10). Abundant living is the result of curbing our own desires and impulses by bringing our wills into obedience to God Almighty. Living the outpoured life of a disciple of Christ produces joy, because that is the fruit of the God-centered orientation. In other words, God Himself should be our goal for living, says Mrs. Cowman.

> *My goal is God Himself, not joy, nor peace,*
> *Nor even blessing, but Himself, my God;*
> *"Tis His to lead me there, not mine, but His—*
> *"At any cost, dear Lord, by any road!"*

So faith bounds forward to its goal in God,
And love can trust her Lord to lead her there;
Upheld by Him, my soul is following hard
Till God hath full fulfilled my deepest prayer.

No matter if the way be sometimes dark,
No matter though the cost be ofttimes great,
He knoweth how I best shall reach the mark,
The way that leads to Him must needs be straight.

One thing I know, I cannot say Him nay;
One thing I do, I press towards my Lord;
My God my glory here, from day to day,
And in the glory there my great Reward.

How do we begin to learn how to love God in that supreme manner? By letting Him nurture us through His Word.

May this become our prayer of importunity: "Blessed are You, O LORD! Teach me Your statutes. I will meditate on Your precepts and contemplate Your ways. I will delight myself in Your statutes; I will not forget Your word" (Psa 119:12, 15-16).

During that marvelous growth process, God simultaneously enables us to say to those He has entrusted to us, "Come, you children, listen to me; I will teach you the fear of the LORD. The things which you learned and received and heard and saw in me, these do, and the God of peace will be with you" (Psa 34:11; Phil 4:9).

A role model for living life in worshiping submission to our precious God and Savior is the best education we can possibly give our children. Therefore, in that sense, our success as teachers depends upon our success as disciples (Matt 10:24).

All the commandments, Jesus said, are rolled up into two: 1) love God, and 2) love your neighbor.

Now that we have begun to set our relationship with Jesus in right order, we are ready to consider our relationship with our husbands.

Chapter Two

Becoming Nurtured in God's Ways

> *"Wives, submit to your own husbands, as to the Lord. For the husband is head of the wife, as also Christ is head of the church. . . . Therefore, just as the church is subject to Christ, so let the wives be to their own husbands in everything"* (Eph 5:22-24).

In our heavenly Father's eyes, a wife's proper relationship to her husband is a lovely act of worship of Christ. Submission to our husbands, as to the Lord, provides daily opportunities to show Him how much He's worth to us. Faithfulness in this, or the lack thereof, impacts our children as well.

God's way is to follow His principle of the chain of command, or chain of authority. Christ is the head of the church; the husband is the head of the wife; the husband and wife are the heads over their children (Eph 5:22-6:4).

Parents who love God with all their hearts and souls are the Lord's role models. As such, it is our responsibility to demonstrate the respect and devotion God deserves by obeying His commands (Deut 10:12-13). One way is to show respect, devotion, and obedience to our husbands (Eph 5:22). This in turn trains our children to do likewise — toward their earthly father first, whom they can see, and then toward our heavenly Father, whom they can't see.

To the degree that we follow God's pattern there should be peace and harmony in our homes. Balking here causes dissonance and can affect our children's relationship with God. Daughters fail to learn how to be godly wives. Sons never learn what it means to be God's head of the home. Thus, the Lord's name is blasphemed before the world (Titus 2:5), since the marriage union is meant to be a beautiful picture of Christ's love for and authority over His bride, the church (Eph 5:22-33).

Marriage is God's training ground to prepare both husband and wife for greater service. As such, both are in a continual state of flux. Ever changing, each unique personality is used by the Lord as heavenly sandpaper on the other. In the nitty gritty of daily living, our true character comes out, not the one we present to others, but the real us. Learning how to biblically handle that day-in–day-out give and take is the key to a successful marriage and successful child training.

Loving our husbands should be characterized by a great fondness or wifely affection with a genuine desire to please (Titus 2:4), just as the affection Jesus has for us (John 15:12).

This speaks of the type of love Christ demonstrated at Calvary when He sacrificed His own life on our behalf. His sacrifice involved the highest form of loving possible. Agape love is based not upon emotions (warm fuzzies or feelings) but on a commitment of the will to act in the best interest of another. In other words, demonstrating a great fondness for our husbands with a genuine desire to please involves voluntary self-sacrifice. Such a sacrifice should depend, not upon what they do or do not do, but upon our commitment to God to always attempt to act in our husbands' best interest. Loving as Christ loved us is in their best interest. To the degree we are faithful to that commitment, we should see a corresponding strengthening in our relationship with both God and our husbands.

This speaks of mature love in contrast to immature. For example, love does not mean the same thing to a child as it does to us. To a child, love means "You do nice things for me. Since I love me, therefore I love you."

When we do not do the nice things our children think we ought to do for them, they may respond with a red-faced "I hate you!" Some adults still know only this Hollywood-style love, which responds only to what someone else does for us or how he makes us feel. When the feelings stop, so does the marriage. That is not God's way.

"But, you don't know my husband," you say. "I live with Attila the Hun!"

To make a point as gently as possible, let's playfully exaggerate a disgruntled wife's description of a typical evening in Attila's home, which is, from her perspective, in Lower Slobovia:

> In walks Attila, just home from the hunt. Wearing his favorite tattered animal skin, scraggly beard and all, he sprawls on his favorite over-stuffed pile of skins and growls. "Hey, wench! Get me a drink! And throw some extra meat on the fire! I'm hungry as a bear! While you're at it, can't you shut those brats up? I've had a hard day at the hunt!"
>
> "Yes, my lord," I reply sweetly. After I serve him the finest meal possible, massaging his massive shoulders while he eats, he belches profusely, tosses leftover dinosaur bones on my freshly swept cave floor and passes out for the evening — without even a grunt of thanks!

But then there are always two sides to a story. Here's Attila's perspective:

> Returning from a faithful day at the hunt, I call out sweetly, "Darling, I'm home!" Walking into what is supposed to be my castle, I see the typical old dungeon — spider webs clinging to the cave roof, dirt not swept for a month, garbage piling up under a rock, kids fighting over their pet tarantula, etc. And

the love of my life? A sight for sore eyes: there, sprawled all over her favorite pile of skins, her long stringy hair tangled from weeks of neglect, wearing an outdated, soiled, and smelly animal skin, gnawing on last night's leftovers, she tosses the bones over her shoulder, wipes her once ruby-red lips with the back of her hand, burps, then replies, "Whatta ya want? Nag! Nag! Nag!" Then I learn that she hasn't even started the fire for our evening meal together!

To the wife, he's Attila the Hun; to the husband, she's Attilette the Hunness. Such lack of consideration on the part of both husband and wife stems from not loving as Christ has loved us. Failure to resolve problem areas is often the result of blaming the other person rather than accepting individual responsibility.

It is the task of the Holy Spirit, not the wife, to convict a husband of his sin problems. We are therefore free to concentrate on our own. The other good news is that, even if a husband *does* resemble Attila, submission to him as to the Lord becomes a sanctified state (Eph 5:26). Through Attila's insensitivities, God can teach us how to be responsible for our own attitudes. The more we respond properly, the stronger our marriages are likely to become.

Consider Sarah when Abraham really "blew it" in his leadership.

D URING A TIME OF FAMINE, she and Abraham went to Egypt. Because Sarah was so beautiful, Abraham feared the Egyptians would kill him to get her. Rather than trust God's protection, Abraham whined, "Please say you are my sister, that it may be well with me for your sake, and that I may live because of you." Sarah obeyed and, because of her beauty, was taken to Pharaoh's house, and Abraham was treated well for her sake. However, the Lord sent great plagues upon Pharaoh's house because of Sarah.

Though Abraham didn't protect her, God did.

She was not physically defiled. God worked that bad situation for good by having Pharaoh send Abraham and Sarah away, laden with riches (Gen 12:10-20).

Sarah's walk wasn't perfect. Nevertheless, God thought enough of it to present it to us as a godly example of faith and good works (1 Pet 3:6). Her faith and good works were centered upon her submissive relationship to Abraham, trusting God to lead through him. God directed Sarah through her husband, and He'll direct us through ours. God, in His mercy, often gives both the husband and wife peace about particular decisions. At other times, He speaks only to our husbands. These are the times that try wives' souls. Again, consider Sarah.

> *"Guess what! We're moving!" Abraham says as he enters their tent. "Jehovah spoke to me today and told me to pack up and go!" Being a woman, Sarah's emotions shoot off in a dozen directions at once. "Move? But what about our family . . . and friends? We'll have to start all over. . . ." Her will, however, helps her to respond: "Well, my lord, where is it Jehovah told you to move?" Then comes the real test. "Beats me," he shrugs. "All I know is He'll tell us when we get there."*

Play the scene in your kitchen for fullest impact. Your husband calls at lunchtime and says, "Hi honey! Listen, I just wanted you to know that I've quit my job. How about calling the moving company to come pack up our stuff? The Lord spoke to me today and told me we're to move. But don't ask me where. He'll let us know when we get there."

What would be your likely reaction? Tough test, huh?

It is not easy to trust God to lead through our husbands. And it is even harder when we believe we are right biblically. But, if we stiffen our necks and dig in our heels, even if we are right, we are wrong.

Some of us may face this type of test when it comes to providing a Christian education for our children. Because mothers are more intuitive than fathers when it comes to children's needs, we are usually the first to identify the importance of biblical education.

IN RESPONSE TO THAT, more and more are feeling called to home school, especially during the formative years. Others believe that utilizing the gifts of the brethren in a Christian school can best meet their family's needs. How should a husband be approached about this? And what do we do if he disagrees? I believe the first thing to do is spread everything out before the Lord in prayer. For our husbands' hearts are in the hand of the Lord (Prov 21:1). Then ask Him for a submissive spirit and wisdom to know the right moment to make an appeal to your husband. As God leads, present your reasoning as sweetly as possible. Then let go, and let God direct.

In moments like these, you can thwart your husband's growth by belittling him and his decision-making ability, or you can build him up by saying, "Honey, I'll pray that God directs you in this decision. For whatever it's worth, I felt it was important to share my heart with you." Through such an approach, you're exhorting him to seek the best Source for wisdom. You are also giving him the benefit of your woman's intuition while at the same time recognizing his God-given authority.

If your husband grants permission to enroll your child in a Christian school kindergarten or to home school for a season, but his attitude is less than enthusiastic, praise God that you do have permission. Then, faithfully follow your convictions with a gentle spirit and continue to pray that the Lord will open your husband's eyes to see the value of God-centered, God-purposed education. In the meantime, be careful that you don't push your child to achieve just to prove you are right!

What if he does not recognize the need for Christian education? Should you get out the boxing gloves? If your husband says "No," accept that decision in a godly spirit. Be careful, because emotions can get in the way of proper responses. If we obey, but with a wrong attitude, it is not obedience at all. You could end up arguing, which is not God's way. The Lord says that it is better to "dwell in a corner of a housetop, than in a house shared with a contentious [quarreling] woman" (Prov 21:9).

A FRIEND OF OURS, who has a terrific sense of humor, actually demonstrated that verse to his wife. When she would not get off his case about something, to make a point, he dramatically climbed to their rooftop. There he sat until she cooled off, which was rather rapidly, considering the ridiculous circumstances.

Just as you want your children to accept your decisions with a proper spirit, so your husband desires that from you. When he's wrong, God will take care of it. (Your test is to resist trying to straighten your husband out for Him.) Remember, God is ultimately in control over your husband's decisions, working even the bad ones for good (Rom 8:28). Continue to pray that God will change your husband's heart. Keep on keeping on in a submissive spirit. That spirit may be the very key God uses to unlock your husband's heart.

In the matter of submission, as well as in many other areas, we have a constant battle with our emotions. When our emotions are under control, they are beautiful, as evidenced in a mother's tender love for her children. But, like Eve, we are also prone to being deceived. Adam knew full well what he was doing; Eve did not (1 Tim 2:13-14; 2 Cor 11:3). As men often view it, women make mountains out of molehills, blow things out of proportion, over-react and act out of impulse.

As an example, we will return to our friends, the Huns:

> *Attila is due home at 5:30 P.M., and he is always punctual. Around 5:45, he is not there; a nagging uneasiness creeps into your mind. By 6:00, still no Attila; worry begins. Perhaps your mind pic-*

tures him lying along a path somewhere, the victim of a wild animal attack. By 6:30, when he is still not home, panic sets in: "Maybe I ought to get my club and go out looking for him!" A few minutes later, Attila, who had been unable to locate a carrier pigeon to send a message, enters the cave and very innocently says, "Hi, honey! I'm home!" You respond, "Home! Where have you been??? Don't you know I've been worried sick about you!! . . . etc., etc." By then, you're so emotionally worked up that it takes two hours to calm down before you're even able to listen to his innocent explanation.

Something like that happened to me several years ago. Ed failed to come home all night. I had heard nothing from him. Since he was then driving 75 miles one way to work along isolated country roads, I had to fight panicky thoughts. Throughout the night, I awakened periodically.

"Dear Lord," I pleaded, "please watch over him, wherever he is!"

Around 8:00 a.m., Ed finally called, saying, "Doreen, I hope you weren't worried! I just wasn't able to get to a phone."

Relief set in, then hilarious laughter as I heard an excuse that I'll bet no other wife has ever heard. "I was sent out on a job to the Alabama boondocks where I've been installing background music at a hog farm all night!"

The point I've been trying to make is that our emotions are our biggest obstacles. We often make decisions without thinking. Therefore, in His wisdom, God placed husbands over us for our protection. A logical cut-and-dry approach to life provides a counterbalance to a purely emotional one. On the other hand, emotional, womanly intuition can provide valuable insights for a husband. Thus, both lives blend together in one flesh (Eph 5:31).

Yet, even though we are meant to be one flesh with our husbands, neither can meet the other's needs perfectly. So we shouldn't expect it. Because the makeup of men is entirely different, they will never be able to identify with our emotional struggles. Nor can we identify with our husbands' struggles. There is a God-ordained reason for that. You see, the Lord intends Himself to be the only One who can fulfill either the husband or the wife.

More than our husbands ever could, God longs for a personal relationship with us. He wants to hear about our heartaches, help us with sin problems, provide wisdom, and meet our physical needs.

KEEPERS OF THE CAVE

Since we have already touched on the subject of our "caves," let us talk about loving our husbands by being good homemakers (Titus 2:4).

From a husband's perspective, the dungeon look is out; the castle look is in. This is true even if he sometimes acts like a cave man. To us, the home our husbands provide might seem more like an actual cave in Lower Slobovia. But, "be it ever so humble, there is no place like home." Regardless of the quality of the dwelling, we can always improve the atmosphere.

Ed and I once lived in a cave-type apartment. The only one we could afford near Chanute Air Force Base was a converted barn. Rent and utilities cost only $65. For that sum, we were entertained by fire-eating dragons (electrical outlets which commonly shot out sparks of fire). The decor could not be beat (e.g., faded sheets for window drapes). Our landlady never restricted the "pets" (cockroaches actively stalking their prey at night). Nor did our guests seem to mind having to walk through our bedroom to get to the kitchen. However, sharing one bathroom with two other apartments did make the great outdoors quite a temptation at times. (No hot bath by 5:00 P.M.? Forget it!)

We had to learn to be content. Adding inexpensive drapes did wonders for the place. So did a small flower arrangement, throw pillows, and bug spray! A sense of humor helped us survive both the apartment and our old '46 Plymouth (bullet hole in the front window, hood tied down with a rope, side window splintered in pieces, would not go over 25 mph). The atmosphere was one of focusing on what we had, rather than on what we did not have.

Keeping a neat and orderly house, operating within wise budget guidelines and preparing nutritious meals are also aspects of loving our husbands. The first step is to stay in the home. No one else can quite fill our shoes like we can. The Greek word translated "keeper-at-home" in the KJV or "homemaker" in the NKJV primarily means "a stayer-at-home." Contrary to popular belief, effectively guiding our households is a marvelous blessing.

Being a good housekeeper is a matter of having a balanced perspective. For many years I had a plaque on the wall which said, "Our house is clean enough to be healthy, but dirty enough to be comfortable." To me, that represented balance. In other words, we should guard against being such perfectionists that no one can comfortably live in the home. If we do not, the house can become a god itself. We should also avoid the opposite extreme in which no one even wants to live there because it is so neglected.

If you are not already a good budgeter, ask the Lord to teach you how to operate within guidelines established by your husband.

In our home, after trying different approaches, a household allowance proved to work best. Ed gives me a flat sum bi-weekly, which I then use to make the house payment and pay for utilities, food, and clothing. He keeps a portion beyond my household allowance for his expenses. Neither has to ask the other for funds. We are responsible for our own realm of budgeting.

In this materialistic age, sometimes young married couples want to start off with everything their parents have. That attitude can pile up debt fast and put a real strain on a marriage. Few can begin at the same standard of living they just left. It took parents years to get what they have. Part of the fun of young marriage is setting goals and working toward them together. In the meantime, part of our training is to learn to be content. Contentment is a matter of choice. It is selfish and insensitive to live beyond our husbands' means. We should look upon tight finances as an opportunity to learn to trust God to meet every need.

Credit card buying can be like telling the Lord we are not willing to wait until He can provide. On occasion, a credit card can meet a real need, if we use it wisely. For that reason, I prefer the American Express card, because the full amount is due each month. That way, I am not tempted to spend what I do not have.

Through prayer, you'll be surprised at how many sales God can lead you to that offer discounts as high as 70–80%. One Christmas, when funds were extremely limited, I was having difficulty finding a gift for Ed. Imagine my delight when I spotted a lovely tie on a sales rack at Sears for only five cents! Things like this have become so common over the years that our family policy has become to "buy nothing unless it is on sale." It is too much joy watching the Lord direct in this area.

Even in grocery shopping, it can be fun looking for the best deals. For example, big quantities do not necessarily mean big savings. A purse calculator is handy for figuring out the unit price of various sizes offered. Make selections based upon the best price, taking into consideration whether or not you can use up the item before it spoils. Inexpensive but nutritious meals are usually healthiest. A good resource for knowing how to fix healthy, reasonably priced meals is the Mennonite *More-with-Less Cookbook* by Doris Janzen Longacre (Scottdale, PA: Herald Press, 1976). An especially favorite book of mine is *Set for Life* by Jane P. Merrill and Karen M. Sunderland (Sunrise Publishers, P.O. Box 1264, Burley, ID 83318, [208]438-4530).

Their principles for achieving and maintaining good health are very sound.

If we do not safeguard our family's health now, they could eventually hear a physician rebuke: "You're too far gone . . . I'm putting you on the 'Yuck-Ptooie!' diet!" If you are not good at meal planning, you can find books or get help from friends. Providing a balanced diet is an extremely important way of biblically loving our husbands and children. Remember, their physical lives are at stake.

God is love and order. Therefore, our homes should be run in an orderly manner (1 Cor 14:40 principle). Managing a household effectively involves "wisdom applied to practice," exercising wise stewardship over both time and resources, both of which belong to God. This is all part of learning to be sober, thus cultivating sound judgment and prudence (Titus 2:4, KJV). And Titus 2:5 admonishes us to be discreet, or to curb our feelings.

The admonition to make wise and prudent decisions also applies to how we take care of ourselves. Part of pleasing our husbands involves paying attention to our appearance.

Every day, our husbands see sharp-looking gals at work. If the home fires aren't kept burning, the hearth gets cold, and a husband could fall prey to a young lady with a better-tended fire.

Perhaps you are such a natural beauty that even when getting up in the morning you look like you just stepped out of the beauty parlor. I am not. For me, looking attractive takes effort. But it's worth it to love my husband by looking neat, well-groomed, and being pleasantly scented. In other words, we should look like someone nice to come home to.

Wisdom and Prudence travel in company with Temperance and Modesty. Too much emphasis on the outward appearance is costly, a time-waster, and can be just plain vain, as in "Mirror mirror on the wall, who's the fairest of them all?" An excessive focus on outward appearances also runs the risk of creating temptation. The way we dress can either communicate godly modesty or a "come-and-get me" invitation, even if we do not intend to do so.

With all the glorification sex gets through the media, both men and women are regularly bombarded with temptation. In fact, I am told that this is the No. 1 battle men face. A Christian marriage seminar speaker once stated, "Men think with their glands; women think with their hearts." For that reason, it is not biblically loving to our husbands to dress in a way which entices other men. Titus 2:5 warns young women to be chaste, meaning "clean, sacred, blameless, or holy."

Because of opposite natures when it comes to sex, the physically intimate side of marriage can really test our character. Jack and Carole Mayhall in *Marriage Takes More Than Love* say that "a man is like an electric light bulb — you flip a switch and on he goes. A woman is more like an electric iron — you flip a switch and it takes a little time to warm up. When you turn it off, it takes a bit of time to cool off too."[4]

Some men lack sensitivity to a wife's sexual needs. They possess "the lovemaking instincts of a frog."

Hubby comes home, sits down, relaxes, has a good meal, reads the evening paper, plays with the kids awhile, takes a bath and goes to bed. The wife goes through the same basic routine, and she goes to bed. Out go the lights . . . And then, suddenly, out of the dark . . . comes a hand."

With no romantic setting or psychological buildup, what should we do? Should we push "the hand" away?

What I am about to recommend can be tough but not impossible. I recommend learning to respond to our husbands anyhow. Part of biblically loving is to focus upon what we can give rather than what we can get in any situation.

On occasions when I am just not in the mood and my husband is feeling frisky, I pray: "Dear Lord, help me to meet his needs. Let this be a time of true satisfaction for him." And God is faithful. If we lovingly respond to our husbands' needs, they'll more likely be open to later gentle communication from us concerning how to better meet our own.

Along this same line, we should be sensitive to how frequently our husbands' makeups require release of their "urges." If we aren't sensitive enough, or if we play games by withholding sex, we could drive them into the arms of another.

> *"Do not deprive one another except with consent for a time, that you may give yourselves to fasting and prayer; and come together again so that Satan does not tempt you because of your lack of self-control"* (1 Cor 7:5).

Don't think this can't happen to your marriage. One of the godliest families I've known was destroyed when the wife ran away with her pastor. That tragic example can serve as a warning to all of us: ". . . Let him who thinks he stands take heed lest he fall" (1 Cor 10:12). It can all start with spending so much time on outward appearances that we fail to develop "the hidden person of the heart, with the incorruptible beauty of a gentle and quiet spirit, which is very precious in the sight of God" (1 Pet 3:4).

The Greek word translated "meek" in the KJV and "gentle" in the NKJV means "mild, humble, gentle." The same word is used of Christ's character. It has the sense of "power under control" or yielding to meet others' needs. To be quiet in spirit means to be "still (undisturbed), peaceable," a comprehensive tranquility which arises from within. It is the type of spirit which causes no disturbance to others around you.

Among the greatest disturbances we can cause are backbiting, gossip, and slander. Because women love to gab, Satan can use gab sessions to tear down the reputations of others, especially husbands.

Suppose one day you have an argument with your husband. You are angry. Human tendency is to make ourselves look good at the expense of others. Therefore, if the opportunity presents itself, you may feel tempted to blow off steam.

"Boy," you might say, "guess what my husband did to me today!"

After getting it all out of your system, you go home, have time to think and repent. But what about the aftermath?

If you follow "do not let the sun go down on your wrath" (Eph 4:26b), you and your husband will make up. Nevertheless, damage has been done. Long after you have restored fellowship, negative comments about him will linger in the memories of your friends. Each time this happens, your husband's reputation dies a little more. Because of the principle that "your sin will find you out" (Num 32:23), what you have said could get back to him. Think about how badly he would feel. Is that biblically loving?

We should protect our husbands' reputations carefully. God says "a good name is to be chosen rather than great riches, Loving favor rather than silver or gold" (Prov 22:1).

I have always made it a point to never speak about Ed in a negative manner to anyone. When we have problems, we work them out together. No one else needs to know. Focusing on what I appreciate about Ed rather than on things which bug me has deepened my love for him. He has also shown the same consideration toward me.

Here is a good rule of thumb for what is and is not proper to discuss: ask yourself whether the person you are talking to is part of the problem or part of the solution. If neither, then do not discuss it.

Being chaste or pure in our speech is God's expectation at all times. "Let no corrupt word proceed out of your mouth, but what is good for necessary edification, that it may impart grace to the hearers" (Eph 4:29). Telling off-color jokes or laughing at them fits into the corrupt category. So does vulgar, abusive, or sarcastic language. Any language which could hurt someone's feelings should be carefully avoided. Our unceasing prayer should be: "Let the words of my mouth, and the meditation of my heart, be acceptable in Your sight, O LORD, my strength, and my redeemer" (Psa 19:14).

Our speech is a direct result of our thought lives, for "out of the abundance of the heart the mouth speaks" (Matt 12:35). Whatever we meditate upon, we will become (Prov 23:7).

Philippians 4:8 provides a checklist for our thought lives: ". . . Whatever things are true, . . . noble, . . . just, . . . pure, . . . lovely, . . . of good report, if there is any virtue and if there is anything praiseworthy — meditate on these things."

Unless something fits with these criteria, we should not listen to it, view it, think it, or speak it. This is a good rule: "Watch the 'whatevers'!" God's way is to demonstrate power under control. We should be like the Proverbs 31 lady who does her husband "good and not evil all the days of her life" (Prov 31:12).

One good way is learning to be genuinely interested in their concerns. To do that, we need to know those concerns, and that requires good listening skills. It is natural to be thinking about what we're going to say while someone else is talking. But this is listening that is half-hearted and self-centered. We must give our husbands our full attention so that we can hear what they are actually saying and what they are not. If your husband is not a talker, then it is a little harder to minister to his needs. But it is not impossible. Through prayer, the Lord can help you be sensitive to what your husband is not saying that may be troubling him.

The Lord is happy to provide us with ways to show "good" to our husbands. Even a simple thing like greeting him at the door in a fresh outfit with a refreshing drink can say, "I love you, honey. Welcome home!" Once he is settled, gently ask questions about how his day went. Show genuine interest in what he does.

WAIT before discussing any problems of your own day. It can make him feel very special if you and he spend a few minutes alone together before your children are permitted to have their turn. This honors him in front of your children as head of his home and also gives him a chance to relax.

Children should not come first; husbands should.

Children do not make a family. They only expand it for awhile. From the moment of each child's birth, a separation process begins. The whole goal of parenting is to rear our children for Christian maturity. This means we are actually training them to leave us. From the moment of marriage, however, a joining process begins with our husbands — physically, spiritually, and emotionally. A top priority must be placed on building that marriage union. Once our fledglings leave the nest, we'll want the remaining years with our spouses to be ones of great joy.

Ed and I survived by using the RHIP Principle of the military (Rank Has Its Privileges). When our children were young, we told them, "Mommy and Daddy get certain privileges right now which you'll also get to enjoy some day when *you* get to be a mommy or daddy."

This meant setting aside "sanity money" (even during tight financial periods) for special times together alone. It need not be much. Going out for coffee and dessert can be precious. Or, leaving the kids with Grandma and Grandpa for the weekend so you can put some extra "spark" in the relationship. Such periods of refreshment makes us better parents as well.

The highest form of doing husbands "good" is encouraging them (not nagging) in the Lord. Young men rarely master their leadership roles before they get married. And we can either stunt their growth or accelerate it. If they do not provide family devotions, we should not usurp their God-given authority (1 Tim 2:12). Instead, we should pray for them. And be patient.

It requires time, patience, and work for men to become godly husbands, just as it does for us to become godly wives.

Because we usually have more time to spend with the Lord, our spiritual growth may be faster than theirs. Approach this very cautiously. We should be careful not to convey to them that we're more spiritual. Sometimes men just have a different way of expressing their faith. Unless they have one of the "utterance" spiritual gifts, men are usually less verbal about their faith than women. If we give the impression that we're more spiritual than they are, our husbands may back off. They may be too embarrassed in front of us because they might think we are looking down on them, and they may not even try to assume their proper spiritual role.

If your husband seems open to suggestions, you might recommend that he use one of the many good family devotionals available today. (Select something with shorter passages to allow for the restlessness of any little children in your household.)

You might also lovingly ask your husband questions about spiritual matters. Seek your husband's wisdom on what you should do in troublesome situations and what scriptural principles he thinks might apply. As you do, pray that the Holy Spirit will prompt him to find the answers. If he does not respond as you think he ought or not at all, do not be unkind.

Biblically loving him involves waiting patiently for God's timing for your husband's spiritual growth. In the meantime, ask the Lord to meet the ache in your own heart whenever no spiritual bond exists with your husband. (In fact, that can be one of His greatest tools for your own personal growth. Truly, God does all things well!)

If you are not married to a Christian, this is what the Bible calls an "unequal yoke." Many of the principles already mentioned still apply because they are based upon your responsibility.

All wives, not only those married to believers, are to "be submissive to your own husbands, that even if some do not obey the word, they, without a word, may be won by the conduct of their wives . . ." (1 Pet 3:1). God requires cheerful submission and loving reverential respect, whether he's good or bad. If you cannot respect the person, respect his position as head of your home. Serving his needs as you would the Lord makes this relationship more bearable.

Unbelievers very carefully observe the lives of those they think simply profess "religion." I have seen God grant some spectacular miracles in unequal marital yokes. But they began with the wife's willingness to do things God's way. At times, relationships were indeed tough. But obedience to God developed patience, proven character, and unshakable confidence in Jesus Christ (Rom 5:3-5). The willingness of wives to sacrifice their lives to God first and then for their husbands so changed their character that Christ used it to save their husbands.

Marriage is a commitment which declares: "You may leave me, but I'll never leave you." When both partners commit themselves to that, they work on the problems until they find God's solutions. Neither bails out, because perfect husbands and wives just don't exist. Whether your husband is a believer or unbeliever, biblically loving him begins with a matter of the will, operating in obedience to Jesus Christ.

TRAINING CHILDREN TO LOVE THEIR FATHER

Wives and children should willingly commit themselves to pleasing God by pleasing Daddy. And, above all, Daddy deserves respect.

Since man was created in God's image, his need for and right to respect is similar to the Father's right to reverence. One might say that the male ego is, in a sense, God-given. Therefore, husbands' egos should be handled gently.

Training children to respect Daddy is a key to developing reverence toward their heavenly Father. We can begin by not allowing children to "talk back" to him. They should never be permitted to speak disrespectfully (even if he acts poorly). That also means our conversation should build rather than tear down his image in our children's minds.

Respect, love, and obedience go hand in hand. If children respect their father, they'll obey him. Eventually, they'll understand that obeying gives proof of love for Daddy. Teaching obedience toward Daddy (whom they *can* see) prepares them to obey God (whom they *cannot* see).

In time, they will discover that joy is a by-product of obedience. Our heavenly Father rejoices in His children's obedience. The same holds true for an earthly father.

> *"The father of the righteous will greatly rejoice,*
> *And he who begets a wise child will delight in him"*
> *(Prov 23:24).*

Submission to God-given authorities produces order. Orderliness in the home in turn lays the foundation for appreciating God's love for order and detail (1 Cor 14:40). Initially, little ones can be taught to love Daddy by helping us care for his castle. They should keep toys, books, and clothes in their proper place when not in use and keep their rooms in order (beds made, floor clear of debris). They could sweep the sidewalk or take out the trash. This also teaches responsibility. A child who has been trained to be faithful in little things can soon be trusted for bigger ones (Luke 16:10). How well this lesson is learned will determine the child's availability for future service for God.

We should also develop a gentle and quiet spirit in our children. When Daddy comes home from work, the atmosphere should be pleasant, without chaos and screaming. By example, we should train our little ones to speak in soft, conversational tones. Giggling and laughter is certainly proper, and even desirable. Otherwise, we'd create a dungeon atmosphere. Yelling is more appropriate when playing outside than in Daddy's castle. If children are not trained to conduct themselves at home in this manner, how can we expect them to behave in their heavenly Father's house, the local church?

Order also results when children are exposed only to the "whatevers" of Philippians 4:8. Whatever they hear and view can affect their overall behavior. What a child thinks about, he'll gravitate toward. This makes a difference in the type of home Daddy returns to each night. It is thus important to build into our children an appetite for the pure things of life. Learning to guard thoughts and speech is preparation for practicing God's holy presence (1 Pet 1:16).

Learning to give sacrificially can help children understand the love of Calvary. We are to love as He has loved us. Unselfishly giving Daddy a few moments to relax when he gets home is one way to learn this lesson. Since little ones normally love Daddy's arrival home, by waiting for his attention, we will be disciplining them to deny self. This is part of learning how to choose to act in the best interest of another. Remember, agape love is the highest form of loving.

Another example of generosity is to do something for Daddy which requires giving of self. For instance, little girls could pick some flowers for him, prepare a pretty little card, cook something, or bring his slippers or newspaper to him. Boys could pick up the yard, help put Daddy's tools away, or wash the tires on his car. We should go to the Source of Creativity for ideas. What we're talking about is developing a servant's heart. Learning to give in this manner prepares our children to give to God through praise and worship, service to others, financial giving, and time.

Temple maintenance is also a way to show love both for God and an earthly father. Our bodies are holy because they are the temple of the Holy Spirit (1 Cor 3:16-17). While they are still little, we should teach children to have an appearance worthy of God's name. As for loving Daddy, just as moms should look nice to come home to, so should children. This does not mean being dressed in Sunday clothes. But neither should Daddy be greeted with filthy faces, gunky noses, or grimy clothes. In the same manner, children should want to look nice for their heavenly Father when they go to His house, the church.

Stewards are to be found faithful (1 Cor 4:2). A steward is one responsible for the oversight of another's property. Since we are not our own (1 Cor 6:20), we are responsible to faithfully do our very best for God (1 Cor 10:31). From the beginning, little children need to know that. Using minds to learn God's Word and His ways through academics fits into this category. Dads are pleased when their offspring exhibit discipline, trying to learn well. Children will learn to expect the same response from their Father in heaven.

Exercising stewardship over the resources Daddy provides is like saying, "I love you, Daddy! I am thankful for all you do for us!"

Wasting electricity and food and abusing clothing, toys, or books shows ingratitude. It says the money Daddy works hard to earn to buy those things is not appreciated. But the message of waste goes even deeper than that. It is ingratitude to God Himself, who ultimately gives us "every good gift" (James 1:17).

In summary, we become *faithful* disciples by feeding on the Word of God and *virtuous* disciples by following the ways of God. But how do we become *knowledgeable* disciples?

God Himself provided us with a pattern for that too. But, just as the devil tempts us with the counterfeit faith of humanism and the counterfeit virtue of feminism, so he has tempted us with the counterfeit knowledge of secularism.

Chapter Three

God-Centered vs. Man-Centered Education

> *"Be ever on your guard lest there shall be some-one who leads you astray through his philosophy, even futile deceit, which is according to the tradition of men, according to the rudimentary teachings of the world, and not according to Christ. . . . because our wrestling is not against flesh and blood, but against the principalities, against the authorities, against the world rulers of this darkness, against spirit forces of perniciousness in heavenly places" (Col 2:8; Eph 6:12, Wuest).*

Have you ever heard anyone refer to the Bible as our "Owner's Manual"? In a sense, that is true. Everything God does, everything He creates, is done according to a plan.

The world was created according to a plan. God gave Noah a specific plan for building the ark. He gave Moses a specific plan for building the tabernacle in the wilderness. He gave Solomon specific plans for building the temple. The priestly garments were designed according to God's plan. There is a plan for our salvation. God does nothing haphazardly.

Is it likely then that God has a plan for education?

HEBREW EDUCATION

In the Garden of Eden, God designed the family as His most important educational agency. The Hebrew people understood that fact. His instructions to parents were "to whet the intellectual appetites of their children. They were to sharpen their minds, prompting questions which would create teachable moments so that instruction in the faith of Israel might be given."[5]

They understood that all knowledge comes from God. Therefore, the aim of education was to understand Him and His work better.

Hebrew education combined the two essentials of learning and doing.

"Along with their religious training," explains Frank Gaebelein, "sons were taught a trade by their fathers; daughters learned household arts from their mothers. Both sexes were taught to read."[6]

Until the time of the exile, home and school were one. God used the tragedy of the exile to "work all things according to the counsel of His will" (Eph 1:11b).

Maynard Hatcher, a free-lance writer who has made the study of ancient near-Eastern literature and history his avocation for more than 35 years, writes:

> In Babylonia, miracles occurred. . . . The Babylonians were tolerant. They permitted the captive Judeans considerable freedom, including religious liberty. . . . In this environment a tremendous literary activity ensued. Gradually, the concept began to take hold that a fitting and suitable replacement for the lost temple and its practices was to study — to learn. . . . It became incumbent on every male Jew to invest time and energy in this endeavor of learning — subjecting himself to the teaching of the learned scribes so that he and his household might be devoted to God and his Law. This was his sacrifice. . . . This, then, is what Ezra brought to the Jerusalem under restoration.[7]

IN THE RESURGENT JUDAH, education of children became a matter of the most extreme intensity. In the home, it was the sacred duty of the fathers. In the community, teachers known as scribes or rabbis performed this sacred function. God's people were beginning to understand that "earthly kingdoms were fallible but the Law (Torah) was the portable fatherland of every Jew. For this to be the case, the Law was to be continuously and unremittingly injected, as it were, into the child beginning with his mother's milk. . . . We start with scripture. We do not tack it on."

As a defense against the encroaching pagan Greek culture, schools began to emerge in the 5th century B.C. However, instruction of young children basically remained in the hands of parents until 75 B.C., when elementary education became compulsory.

The Synagogue became the first really formal educational institution of the Hebrews. Because Scripture was the only textbook, these schools became known as "houses of the book." In addition, by the time of Christ, the oral Talmud was securely in place. Jesus used many of its teachings as illustrations for His own. At the time of Christ, school was in session throughout the entire year. During children's formative years, it was considered essential to inculcate the Torah in their lives. Such study was "likened to an inscription in fresh ink upon newly-pressed papyrus—it remained indelible forever."

Education began in infancy. Timothy's training by his mother and grandmother apparently followed Jewish tradition. From infancy, Timothy knew the Scriptures (2 Tim 3:15). This meant that he had an experiential knowledge of them. They meant something to him.

For a moment, consider Timothy's background. He came from a mixed marriage. His Jewish mother, Eunice, was a believer. But his father was a Greek (Acts 16:1). Eunice's mother, Lois, had trained her well. They are a positive example of the proverb, "Like mother, like daughter." (See Ezekiel 16:44 and 2 Timothy 1:5.) Even though his father was an unbeliever, God richly blessed the training Timothy received from his mother and grandmother.

As soon as a child first started to speak, it was common for the father to teach him to repeat selected Bible verses. This reveals the sages' "appreciation of the cultivation of a child's imitative, mechanical faculties even before the attainment of understanding."

A noteworthy Talmudic passage "informs us how the infants were taught the Hebrew alphabet. To assist the memory and to make the task of learning more attractive, words were associated with letters; but most important of all, the alphabet was employed as a medium of religious and ethical instruction," for example, according to *Everyman's Talmud* by A. Cohen:

> *K is the first letter of "holy" and R of "wicked."*
> *Why does K turn its face away from R? The Holy*
> *One, blessed be He, says, "I cannot look upon the*
> *wicked." Why is the foot of K turned towards R?*
> *The Holy One, blessed be He, says, "If the wicked*
> *repent, I will place a crown upon him like My*
> *own." Why does the leg of K hang detached? If the*
> *wicked repent, he can enter through the opening*
> *(and so find himself within the "Holy One").* [8]

The methodology used was to recite such lessons by rote in unison. The purpose of teaching infants the alphabet was to prepare them for the beginner's curriculum, which "consisted of only one subject, learning to read and write Hebrew, the language of the Holy Writings." At that time there was a pedagogical (teaching) rule that "at five years the age is reached for studying the Bible. . . ."

When the beginner's curriculum was initiated, the teacher didn't worry whether pupils were capable of grasping the subject matter. First came memorization of a lesson, and then the explanation.

The teacher tried to stimulate their intellectual appetites by getting them to ask questions about the lesson. If a child was unable to ask the right questions, the teacher "opened his mouth." In other words, he put the question in his mouth. Giving a small reward of fruit, raisins, or cakes at the end of each day's lessons was meant as a practical application of Psalm 119:103: "How sweet are thy words unto my taste! yea, sweeter than honey to my mouth."

Until age 13, a pupil usually attended the Bible school. By then, he had a good foundation in the religion, history, sacred language, and literary heritage of his people. He was thus considered ready to undertake practical work to become a farmer, craftsman, or merchant. Girls were considered adults at 12, boys at 13. At that point, the father no longer had to teach them the Torah and the observance of *mitzvot*. These young adults were now responsible to continue studying on their own, for Hebrews believed that "education is not to be treated as distinct from the inner content of life but as one with it; accordingly, Torah study is not to be limited to a certain age but to continue throughout one's life. . . ."

In contrast to children of today, Hebrew children were reared for maturity. If parents had been faithful to instill delight for God and the study of His Word, their children would normally continue lifelong learning. However, when parents failed to do so, as history records, their children went the way of the world.

As an educational institution, the home "would become the hallmark of the Jewish people." Despite its imperfections, the status of education at the time of Christ was considered a "unique cultural phenomenon—the approximation of pedagogical achievement to the ideal, not only in the attainments of exceptional individuals but also in the numbers of outstanding contemporary personalities."

Mr. Gaebelein concludes: "It is in its devotion to the Word of God and its relation to life that ancient Hebrew education has relevance for Christian education in modern times. Not only are the Torah (Pentateuch) and the Book of Proverbs the oldest educational handbooks, but the entire OT stands along with the NT as the chief sourcebook for an authentically Christian education."

COLONIAL EDUCATION

Colonial America saw a resurgence of educating children to delight in God and lifelong learning. The principles used by early Hebrews to achieve success were revived by Colonial parents who purposed to train their children so they would so appropriate "God's message of redemption in Christ Jesus that all of life comes to be lived by them in obedience to the Scriptures."

Particularly in New England, "born into a religious atmosphere, reared in religious ways, surrounded on every side by religious influences, they could not escape the impress of deep religious feeling; they . . . had a profound familiarity with the Bible." It was the "universal child's book of that day, says author Alice Morse Earle in her 1899 edition of *Child Life in Colonial Days*."9

The family of the seventeenth century "that read the words of the small Geneva Bibles in the home circle, or poorer folk who listened to the outdoor reading thereof, heard a voice that they had longed for and waited for and suffered for, and that their fathers had died for, and a treasure thus acquired is never lightly heeded."

In the early Colonial period, education began in the home, and, as with the Hebrews, at a very early age. The seventeenth century was known for its records "of the precocity of children [both religious and intellectual], preserved for us many times." Learning to read between the ages of two and four was common.

When Mrs. Jane Turell "was three years old she could recite the greater part of the *Assembly's Catechism*, many of the psalms, many lines of poetry, and read distinctly; at the age of four she 'asked many astonishing questions about divine mysteries.'"

Another example of the spirit of the times in regard to juvenile education is found in the letters of Mrs. Pinckney. She wrote asking her sister to purchase a toy similar to our alphabet blocks for her three-month-old son. Her goal was to teach him his letters by the time he could speak. Later, Mrs. Pinckney wrote her sister that he could identify his letters in any book without hesitation and was able to spell before he was two years old.

Martha Laurens "could, in her third year, 'read any book.'" Joseph T. Buckingham "declared that when he was four years old he knew by heart nearly all the reading lessons in the primer and much of the *Westminster Catechism*." In his memoirs he stated that he "read the Bible through at least a dozen times before he was sixteen years old."

The following instructions from a children's book once more shows the Colonial spirit toward early education:

> *As soon as the child can speak, let him stick a pin through the page by the side of the letter you wish to teach him. Turn the page every time and explain the letter by which means the child's mind will be so fixed upon the letter that he will get a perfect idea of it, and will not be liable to mistake it for any other. Then show him the picture opposite the letter and make him read the name thereof.*

Sometimes, parents taught children as young as three to read Latin words as soon as they could English ones. Timothy Dwight, President of Yale College, is reported to have learned the alphabet at a single lesson, could read the Bible before he was four years old, and taught it to his friends.

Colonial children learned the alphabet as Hebrew children had. Like the Talmud, the famous *New England Primer* taught the alphabet through a system of spiritual rhymes.

Consider these representative rhymes for *Aa* and *Bb*: "In Adam's fall, We sinned all"; "Thy life to mend, God's Book attend."

The *New England Primer* also contained selections from the Bible, the Lord's Prayer, the Apostles' Creed, children's prayers, and exhortations to children to seek fervently and respectfully to know God and obey His truths.

The teaching of spiritual and moral truths through the medium of academics was also recommended by Charles H. Spurgeon, who has often been referred to as the great "preacher of preachers":

> *As we sow we reap. Let us expect our children to know the Lord. Let us from the beginning mingle the name of Jesus with their A B C. Let them read their first lessons from the Bible. It is a remarkable thing that there is no book from which children learn to read so quickly as from the New Testament: there is a charm about that book which draws forth the infant mind.*

Colonists, however, did not conceive of education in the way we do today. Rarely did they confuse schooling with education. They considered education to be an individual family responsibility. Most children, at an early age, learned to read, write, and figure in the home. Girls almost certainly would be trained in housekeeping. Boys were taught many of the tasks of making a living. Apprenticeship under a master was common.

Little time was spent in play in relationship to work, due to the belief that idle hands are the devil's workshop. Many of the games played in the Colonial period originated from religious observances. Common toys of that era were dolls, drums, watches, a pair of scales, hobby horses, skates, and a good jackknife for boys. It was "not until October, 1771, that a pleasure-filled item appeared, 'Boys' Marbles.'"

Grammar schools served students ranging from seven to fourteen or fifteen (similar to today's elementary and junior high). Admittance was based upon having already learned to read and write. Once enrolled, studies were devoted to learning the Latin language and literature written in it. This was the "college prep" course of that day.

"The religion of these Calvinist Puritans demanded that they be literate," comments Neil Postman. The "schooling of the young was understood by the colonists not only as a moral duty but as an intellectual imperative. . . . And it is clear that growth in literacy was closely connected to schooling."[10] In fact, Colonial students achieved the highest literacy rate in the world.

The disciplined way of life enhanced the intellectual development of the colonists.

"The Founding Fathers were sages, scientists, men of broad cultivation, many of them apt in classical learning, who used their wide reading of history, politics, and law to solve the exigent [urgent] problems of their time." Their solid scriptural foundation provided the basis for applying biblical criteria to every sector of life. It is no surprise that such a disciplined religious culture produced leaders who contributed greatly to America's Christian character.

Annals of the American Pulpit, Vol. I, evaluates two hundred religious leaders of the Colonial period. Very early in life they commonly showed a strong delight in learning, coupled with a deep commitment to God. What set these leaders apart and made them so great was that this delight and commitment continued throughout their lifetimes.[11]

Increase Mather (1639-1723), for example, was considered intellectually precocious in his early childhood. He "did not decline the usual innocent diversions of children, yet he greatly outstripped all his school-mates in the acquisition of knowledge," so much so, that he entered Harvard at age twelve. His mother is especially credited with conducting his moral and religious education with the utmost care. He maintained his intellect until past eighty. His funeral was "more numerously and honourably attended, than any funeral in the Province had ever been."

The delight Dr. Mather experienced in lifelong learning was inherited by his son, Cotton (1662-1728). From his earliest childhood, Cotton evidenced a unique love for books and learning. He entered the free school in Boston at an early age. By the time he was twelve, he had begun studies at Harvard. By age fourteen, it was common for him to read fifteen chapters or more of the Bible every day. It was reported that "his learning was probably more varied and extensive than that of any other person in America." Cotton saw something spiritual in all the common activities of daily life because his heart was so devoted to God.

Another fine example of lifelong learning which began in the earliest years is Joseph Sewall, D.D. (1688-1769). Dr. Sewall was the son of the Hon. Samuel Sewall, a Chief Justice of the Superior Court of Massachusetts. Early in life, his mind was brought under a religious influence. In his father's published *Diary,* Joseph was reported as "toddling off to his first day of school at the age of two years and eight months." He graduated from Harvard at age nineteen. Dr. Sewall "retained his mental faculties . . . til he reached the period of four score years." His life was "distinguished above almost any other man of his time for devotional fervour and simple and earnest engagedness in his work."

Jonathan Edwards (1703-1758) was considered "one of the great lights, not only of his country, but of the world." While "a mere child, [he] exhibited powers of reflection that would have been remarkable, even at a maturer period." It was "the legitimate opening of a mind which had in it the elements of mighty power, and was destined to become one of the brightest glories of the age." His earliest childhood years were a model of docility and obedience, with deep interest in religious things. He had a thirst for knowledge which led him to enter Yale by age thirteen. During the illness which finally claimed his life, his main concern was to "lie passive in the hands of his Heavenly Father."

"Puritan traits and habits lingered in generation after generation and outlived change of environment and mode of living." Why? Because they "developed at an early age a comprehension of religious matters which would seem abnormal to-day, but was natural then." Success (also translated "intelligence") is directly related to a person's relationship to the written and living Word of God (Josh 1:8, Prov 1:7).

SECULARIZATION AND
CONTEMPORARY EDUCATION

By the end of the nineteenth century, a secularization process was well underway. The God of Scripture was being removed from sector after sector.

God's people, like many today, missed the drama of the heavens, the spiritual warfare going on around them (Eph 6:12; 2 Cor 10:3-5). Thinking they were standing, they fell to the traditions of men (1 Cor 10:12).

In fierce opposition to the God-centered, God-purposed education of the Reformation and Colonial periods, a man-centered system steadily took over. The Enlightenment, spearheaded by Jean-Jacques Rousseau (1712–1798), began an all-out move to enthrone man and dethrone God. Francis Schaeffer viewed Rousseau as "the most important influence on modern thought." Rousseau's educational theories are expressed in his book *Emile*, which many consider to be the foundation of modern educational theory.

ROUSSEAU WAS ANTI-INTELLECTUAL. He considered life experiences rather than reason as the basis for gaining knowledge. Opposing bookishness, he advocated educating children's senses instead. This meant replacing learning facilitators such as words and books with those of objects and environment. In modern terms, field trips and demonstrations would have been preferred over reading. Rousseau felt books clutter minds with useless knowledge. Therefore, books were to be kept from children under ages twelve to fifteen.

The outward acceleration of the child by the teacher or parent was thus unacceptable, a concept Rousseau shared with Jean Piaget, a child psychologist who spent 50 years or so at the J. J. Rousseau Institute in Geneva.

Rousseau's philosophy strongly impacted Johann Heinrich Pestalozzi (1746-1827), who in turn discipled Friedrich Froebel (1782-1852). The contemporary idea of "readiness" can be traced back to Pestalozzi.

Pestalozzi and Froebel introduced the use of "the senses" and "freedom to investigate" into a school system previously dominated by discipline, verbalization, memorization, and reading. The curriculum of compensatory education used today as an antidote for cultural deprivation draws heavily from their thinking.

Until age 55, Froebel failed at almost everything he tried. However, in 1837 he started the first kindergarten in Blankenburg, Germany. He gave it the name "kindergarten" "to convey the idea of an environment in which children could grow freely as plants, according to the nature of the child."

By Froebel's time, children's natures were considered innocent. Neither good nor evil, each child was to be free to be his own authority. In contrast, Scripture tells us to restrain children. Left to their own way, they'll grow up in conformity with their sinful natures. Eli was judged severely for failing to restrain his sons (1 Sam 3:13). God's Word teaches that "a child left to himself brings shame to his mother" (Prov 29:15).

Froebel believed that "play is not only the child's primary learning medium, but also his work. Educators should cultivate the spirit of play in a child." ". . . Play is a child's work," said Dr. David Elkind, is now "a kind of motto for contemporary early childhood education."[12] Drs. Gangel and Benson believe that Froebel's play-work philosophy had distinct religious overtones:

> *Play is the highest phase of child develop-*
> *ment . . . play is the purest, most spiritual activity*
> *of man at this stage, and at the same time, typical of*
> *human life as a whole — of the hidden natural life*
> *in man and in all things. . . . It holds the source of*
> *all that is good.* [13]

FROEBEL LAUNCHED A DEFINITE SHIFT in emphasis from a work-play priority to play-work. However, this runs contrary to the pattern God Himself set for us. Six days we are to labor. On the seventh day, we are to rest (Ex 20:9-11).

In his book, *Revolt Against Maturity*, Dr. R. J. Rushdoony explains that "life is not defined by play but by work and dominion." A play-work emphasis is a revolt against order. Author Colleen Dedrick, in an article entitled *Unschooling: The Ungodly Education,* explains:

> *The Scriptures teach us that learning is gaining*
> *or receiving knowledge; receiving instruction; taking*
> *a pattern. Learning is taught under discipline and*
> *discipleship. "Take my yoke upon you and learn of*
> *Me, for I am meek and lowly . . ." (Matt 11:29).*
>
> *Play is doing something for pleasure, recreation or*
> *amusement (Ex 32:6); work is to labor, particularly*
> *physical (manual), or mental, (Gen 2:15-19; 3:23;*
> *1 Thess 4:11).*[14]

In spite of the clarity of Scripture on this subject, Christians nevertheless continued to fail to take dominion and exercise leadership in every sector. This neglect accelerated the final stages of being led astray.

Froebel's kindergarten concept gained a foothold in America by 1873. Kindergartens then became an established part of our educational system, in one form or another.

Early in the twentieth century, the practices of Dr. Maria Montessori (1870-1952) also started to gain a foothold. The prediction that the twentieth century would become the century of the child is often attributed to her. That prediction has come true. The mixing of child-centered education and modern child psychology which began at the turn of the century through seeds planted by Charles Darwin is just one example.

ALTHOUGH MONTESSORI BELIEVED in early reading, she agreed with Froebel in many areas. Thus "the child in her preschool was left to pursue his own interests and free to solve problems without interference." The key to her system at all ages was "freedom from inhibition or the substitution of adult will and way."

Such a view certainly appeals to our sinful natures. However, true freedom is the liberty to do what we ought to do rather than what we want to do. For only where the Spirit of the Lord is can there be genuine liberty (2 Cor 3:17).

Drs. Gangel and Benson believe that Montessori probably had an influence on John Dewey (1859-1952), as did Rousseau, Pestalozzi, and Froebel.

Dewey considered the teacher to be a facilitator, not an imparter of knowledge. Rather than being a succession of studies, the curriculum was to revolve around the child. He argued that we should "begin with the child and from his experience we develop the learning process, rather than superimposing what we believe is important upon the child's experience." The very young child was to learn to view himself as judge and explorer before any system of thought subjugate his mind. This was basic to Dewey's belief that school could wait, a belief which could be traced back to Rousseau and Pestalozzi.

"Experience" vs. "content-centered" education should be examined biblically. "Learning by doing" is important, but it should never exclude other equally valid methods of learning. Focusing upon "learning by doing" subtly shifts children from being *receivers* of what they should learn to becoming *deciders* of what they will learn — and when. The latter puts the child in control rather than the authorities God holds responsible to rear children to Christian maturity. Learning which originates in the learner is child-centered education rather than God-centered.

Learning which originates in the Word of God teaches children the mind of Christ. We are not "free" to gain knowledge according to our own way. God is the one who imparts knowledge to man (Psa 94:10) by combining both learning (content-centered) and doing (practical application).

THE BIBLICAL EDUCATIONAL POSITION was opposed by Dewey. In 1933, he was one of the signers of *Humanist Manifesto I*, the credo of Secular Humanism. The U.S. Supreme Court has declared Secular Humanism to be a religion. It deifies man rather than God. ("If no deity will save us, we must save ourselves.") Samuel Blumenfeld said Dewey was one of "the lethal trio who were to literally wipe out traditional education and kill academic excellence in America."

Dewey and his followers, Blumenfeld said, possessed "a missionary zeal to rebuild American education on a foundation of science, evolution, humanism, and behaviorism. Dewey [a collectivist] identified high literacy as the culprit in traditional education, the sustaining force behind individualism. He wrote in 1898:

> *My proposition is, that conditions — social, industrial, and intellectual — have undergone such a radical change, that the time has come for a thoroughgoing examination of the emphasis put upon linguistic work in elementary instruction. . . .*

The plea for the predominance of learning to read
in early school-life because of the great importance
attaching to literature seems to me a perversion.

"When a nation's leading educational reformers start arguing in favor of illiteracy and inaccurate reading," Blumenfeld said, "and [condemning] an early emphasis on learning to read as a perversion, then we can expect some strange results to come from our education process."[15]

He went on to state that "the literary breakdown in this country is no accident. It is not the result of ignorance or incompetence. It has been, in fact, deliberately created by our progressive-humanist-behaviorist educators, whose social agenda is far more important to them than anything connected with academic excellence."

The dichotomy is clear and uncompromising when considered point for point:

GOD-CENTERED EDUCATION vs. MAN-CENTERED EDUCATION

- **God is on the throne; He is Savior and Lord.**
  - ☐ Man is on the throne; he is his own savior.

- **Educate in the mind of Christ. Spiritual and moral truths are taught through academics.**
  - ☐ A child's knowledge, skill, mind, and character is developed in terms which leave God out.

- **Children's natures are sinful; restraint is in order.**
  - ☐ Children's natures are innocent; they should be "free" to explore.

- **Early education, to include reading is wise.**
  - ☐ Books and schools can wait. Early learning is harmful.

- **Educate through a succession of studies combined with practical application. Learning and doing applies.**

☐ Curriculum revolves around the child and his experience. Learning by doing is emphasized.

- **Memorization, verbalization, and reading lay an important foundation.**

  ☐ Educate the senses. Field trips and demonstrations are best.

- **The teacher is an imparter of knowledge, according to each child's needs.**

  ☐ The teacher is a facilitator, according to a child's desires.

- **Work-play priority is important.**

  ☐ Play-work is predominant.

- **Educate for Christian maturity.**

  ☐ Let children be "kids."

God-centered education produces future adults who recognize that this world is a spiritual battleground. Man-centered education produces children in adults' bodies who consider the world as a playground!

By 1955, the successful destruction of academic excellence prompted Rudolf Flesch to write *Why Johnny Can't Read*. That, along with the launching into orbit of Russia's Sputnik I in 1957, "resulted in a frantic search for reasons why American children were behind the Russians in academic Achievement. . . . Achievement began to replace adjustment as the highest goal of the American way of life. . . ."[16]

Dr. Elkind, in *The Hurried Child*, considers this search as an "attack on 'progressive education.'" As a result, parents were flooded in the 1960s with information on the importance of learning during the early years. Tax-supported kindergartens began operation in almost every state. Some included formal instruction in reading and math.

Dr. Elkind quoted Jerome Bruner's famous phrase, "That any subject can be taught effectively in some intellectually honest form to any child at any stage of development." The implementation action of that philosophy during the civil rights movement brought to light the poor performance of disadvantaged children. Since those students were not doing well, educators blamed the homes. Headstart and busing were created to close the educational gap.

Others reacted with a "Super Baby" approach to education. This meant a push-push emphasis from infancy. But pushing children's minds to give them a shot at "the good life" by getting into the best colleges can't satisfy the needs of children's souls. Because of that, overly-stressed kids often escape "by running away, getting into drugs, dropping out of school, becoming delinquent, or simply refusing to perform."

"Sesame Street" was introduced in 1969 as another attempt to find answers to the academic dilemma. It was Froebel's play-work philosophy put in action with puppets. "Sesame Street," writes Neil Postman, "relieved [parents] of the responsibility of teaching their pre-school children how to read — no small matter in a culture where children are apt to be considered a nuisance. . . . 'Sesame Street' was entirely consonant with the prevailing spirit in America. Its use of cute puppets, celebrities, catchy tunes, and rapid-fire editing was certain to give pleasure to the children and would therefore serve as adequate preparation for their entry into a fun-loving culture."

That show is "an expensive illustration of the idea that education is indistinguishable from entertainment." The end result was that children loved school only if it was like "Sesame Street." This impacted them all the way through college.

Teachers, from primary grades through college, are increasing the visual stimulation of their lessons; are reducing the amount of exposition their students must cope with; are relying less on reading and writ-

ing assignments; and are reluctantly concluding that the principal means by which student interest may be engaged is entertainment.

Now, STATE SCHOOLING is like a production-line cafeteria. Students are fed a diet of curriculum-centered entertainment topped off with values clarification, situation ethics, and sex, drug, and death education. The Bible has been barred from our schools, and with it, the values parents and pastors are trying to instill.

The individual needs of children are being overlooked. Factory management schooling has become more like a cattle drive: "Move 'em on out!" Standards are lowered year after year. Children who have not truly passed a grade are often moved on to make room for the next herd. As a result, many "children are being pressured to produce for the sake of teachers and administrators."

The end result is like saying: "The operation was a success, but the patient died." The operation "educate to graduate" succeeded, and the patient (the student) died to lifelong learning. After graduation, studying simply ceases. It is too much work.

The curriculum-centered, entertainment approach to education even filtered into Christian schools. For example, in my early years at Rocky Bayou Christian School, I attended several teacher-training clinics at another well-known, highly successful Christian school. There I received training on ways to make instruction lots more fun in order to better entice children to learn. Workshops at Christian school teachers' conventions also offered the same approach. In comparison to God-centered educational workshops, the "fun" workshops were by far the best supported.

From our children's earliest years, they are being programmed, directly and indirectly, with a world view that fosters a love for all that is in it (1 John 2:16). Yet, God tells us: "Do not love the world or the things in the world. If anyone loves the world, the love of the Father is not in him" (1 John 2:15).

Parental reaction to this fun-and-games approach has helped to give rise to the rapidly growing home school movement in America. Unfortunately, in an attempt to protect their children from the stress of production-line education, some home schooling parents are going back to more child-centered education. They believe early formal learning is the problem. So they favor the "doing" of education over academic learning, especially learning to read. The *laissez faire* outlook on the early years is commonly preferred, refraining from formal schooling until at least the mid-elementary years.

Still others are realizing, "The problem with the factory management system is that it pushes children too much and puts them into a uniform mold. The child-centered systems, in contrast, may not push children enough." Those parents are searching for an alternative to the two extremes.

The key is to get beyond the "when" and "how" issue of education and focus upon the "why" of education. But this is difficult unless you understand the root problem.

The root problem is secularization. When the God of Scripture was removed from education, with Him went its meaningful whole. The vacuum left by Christian parents who failed to pass on the Faith was gradually filled with the traditions of men.

Prior to the twentieth century, according to Os Guinness in *The Gravedigger File*, "where there was faith, however small numerically, it had a characteristic social and cultural influence because it mulishly insisted on applying [God's] rule to all of life. 'If Jesus Christ is not Lord of all, he is not lord at all' could have been the banner under which the faithful soldiered."[17] Their whole way of life was found in Christ Himself.

In contrast, "modern faith, however large it is in numbers (as in America), almost never has this total view. It is secularization which has made the difference." It is now "a historical reality which has happened to modern societies over the last two hundred years." In other words, "God was slowly executed here," says author Allan Bloom, and "it took two hundred years" to do it. Worldly-mindedness of the church allowed such a secularization process to happen.

Christian minds have now become fragmented into sacred-secular thinking patterns. Instead of applying God's rule to all of life, as did genuinely faithful Hebrew and Christian forefathers, there is now "one mind for church, another for the classroom; one for reading the Bible, another for reading the newspaper; one for the world of the family, another for the world of business" writes Guinness.

Therefore, Guinness continues, even though beliefs about the Bible "have rarely been stricter; behavior under it has rarely been looser." As a result, Christianity has deserted the public sphere.

"Sector after sector has been successively freed from the influence of the Christian faith, so that for all practical purposes the heartland of modern society is thoroughly secular. The steely grip of the sacred-secular distinction is now a stranglehold."

Having deserted the battle for the public sphere, it was inevitable that Christians would "pay through the nose for [our] refusal to think," writes author Neil Postman.

> Our politics, religion, news, athletics, education and commerce have been transformed into congenial adjuncts of show business, largely without protest or even much popular notice. The result is that **we are a people on the verge of amusing ourselves to death**. (Emphasis added.)

In *The Closing of the American Mind*, Allan Bloom reveals the results of his study of thousands of students considered as those most likely "to have the greatest moral and intellectual effect on the nation." Bloom laments the traits and habits of these students compared with those he taught around a quarter of a century ago and attributes this change to "the gradual stilling of the old political and religious echoes in the souls of the young."[18] In short: we've lost our Christian heritage!

PROFESSOR BLOOM HAS DISCERNED what many Christians have missed, and that is that the Bible is the source for learning how to look at life as a whole. In the past, "the Bible was the only common culture" which united people from all walks of life. Now, without the Bible, "even the idea of the order of the whole is lost." He blames the family for failing to nurture the students in God's Word. For "the dreariness of the family's spiritual landscape passes belief. . . . children are raised, not educated." He says he's not talking about "unhappy, broken homes that are such a prominent part of American life, but the relatively happy ones." As a whole, parents now "lack self-confidence as educators of their children."

As a result, multitudes of young people are growing up to be "lovers of themselves, lovers of money, boasters, proud, blasphemers, disobedient to parents, unthankful, unholy, unloving, unforgiving, slanderers, without self-control, brutal, despisers of good, traitors, headstrong, haughty, lovers of pleasures rather than lovers of God . . ." (2 Tim 3:2, 4-5).

"To say, 'I've got my rights,' is as instinctive with Americans as breathing," Bloom says, "so clear and evident is this way of looking at things. . . . To sum up, the self is the modern substitute for the soul." Or, as Pastor John Stormer concludes in *Growing Up God's Way*:

> **The homes and family must accept the responsibility for the failures.** *The Bible makes it plain that behavior in life is the result of childhood training — or lack of it. Proverbs 22:6 says: "Train*

up a child in the way he should go: and when he is old, he will not depart from it." (Emphasis added.)[19]

Stormer writes that Dr. Reginald Lourie, President of the Joint Commission on Mental Health of Children, testifying before a U.S. Senate committee in support of a bill to give more governmental control of early childhood education, told why "experts" push for total government control of children. Dr. Lourie said:

> There is serious thinking among child researchers that we cannot trust the family alone to prepare young people for the new kind of world — not only are parents unnecessary, but they are too inept to rear their children.

Perhaps Dr. Lourie is right. But our God says the story does not have to end here.

> "'Yet from the days of your fathers you have gone away from My ordinances and have not kept them. Return to Me, and I will return to you,' says the Lord of hosts" (Mal 3:7).

Chapter Four

God in Reading:
The Foundation of Learning

"... Give attention to reading, to exhortation, to doctrine. Be diligent to present yourself approved to God, a worker who does not need to be ashamed, rightly dividing the word of truth" (1 Tim 4:13; 2 Tim 2:15).

"In the beginning ... God said...." God spoke the universe into existence with words, with language.

"The man said, 'This is now bone of my bones ....'" The first man spoke words, used language to communicate with his Creator and with his wife, with his own kind.

"The Lord said, 'If as one people speaking the same language they have begun to do this [build a city to glorify themselves rather than God], then nothing they plan to do will be impossible for them.'"

God said, the man said. Nothing will be impossible. Words have the power of life and death. By our words we are justified or condemned (Matt 12:37). We overcome the devil by the blood of the Lamb and the word of our testimony (Rev 12:11). And Satan doesn't like any of this. So he set out to keep God's people, indeed, *all* people, from reading, writing, and mastering words.

THE DRAMA UNFOLDS

To get the greatest impact from what transpired, envision yourself sitting in an audience about to watch a scene from the "Drama of the Heavens." As the curtain goes up, God-centered education with its primary emphasis on biblical literacy is fading out. Satan and his forces of darkness are working behind the scenes launching an all-out effort to destroy man's ability to read. The Enlightenment with its resultant secularization process is well under way.

Just as Rousseau, who spearheaded the Enlightenment, tremendously influenced Pestalozzi, Froebel, and Dewey, so he influenced the one who would launch the first attack upon the traditional method of learning to read.

Professor Friedrich Gedike, a German educator, wrote the first look-and-say primer in 1791. Rudolf Flesch reports:

> Herr Professor Gedike was a fervent believer in the educational theories of Jean-Jacques Rousseau. He said teaching should follow nature. Nature presented Man with wholes — a flower, a tree, an animal, a mountain. To learn about those wholes, Man had to analyze what they were made of, going from the whole to its parts. . . . Reading instruction, too [Gedike wrote], should go from the whole — that is, the word to its parts — the letters. [20]

Rather than going from the "what" (the particulars of letter/sound relationships which quickly lead to the whole) as had been done successfully since the time of Moses, Gedike's look-and-say method now reversed that procedure. Even though several other European educators jumped on the band wagon, the look-and-say reading approach failed to fully catch on at that time.

About 45 years later, look-and-say was reinvented in America by Thomas H. Gallaudet, a worker with deaf mutes.

Because they could not hear phonics, he developed a purely visual method of teaching them to read, and he thought it a good way to teach hearing children as well.

In 1836, Gallaudet published his method under the title *A Mother's Primer*. Others followed, using the same principle. One was Mrs. Mary Peabody Mann, the second wife of Horace Mann. In her book, she never even mentioned the alphabet or letters. Nevertheless, her husband still gave it a favorable review.

In 1843, the Manns visited Europe. In an hour's demonstration of the "normal word method" (phonics) by a Prussian teacher, Mann misunderstood what he was seeing as being look-and-say. That, combined with the methods of a few others (including his wife), prompted him to return to this country and make "a frontal attack on the prevailing method of teaching children with the alphabet and bă, bě, bǐ, bŏ, bŭ."

Despite Mann's efforts, however, look-and-say never really caught on until 1881 when George Farnham revised the method by suggesting that children read and write whole sentences from the very beginning of the learning-to-read process. Rather than being thrown out as ridiculous, it was soon widely accepted. That launched an influx of sentence-method or story-method primers. The *Elson Readers,* published by the Scott, Foresman Company, were the forerunners of the "Dick and Jane" series.

Farnham's work set the stage for Colonel Francis Wayland Parker, who Flesch considers as the great national leader of look-and-say. He achieved national recognition as a superintendent of public schools in Quincy, Massachusetts, and then principle of Chicago's Cook County Normal School. After being fired in Cook County, he established a wing using his reading methods at the University of Chicago. There he became internationally recognized.

The "next hero of the look-and-say movement is Edmund Burke Huey, author of *The Psychology and Pedagogy of Reading*, which appeared in 1908. It instantly became the bible of the movement." Mr. Flesch refers to Huey's work as "this strange new **gospel** on how to teach reading."

As the "bible" of the look-and-say movement, Huey's work dealt a deadly blow not only to phonics but also to early reading. No longer were schools to emphasize primary reading skills. Reading itself was not to appear in the early years of school. Whatever phonics was permitted was to be entirely distinct from reading. Reading for the sake of reading as a formal process or end in itself was discouraged. In other words, it was never to be done or thought of as an exercise. It was supposed to be according to the inward interest of the child or for the value of its content. From the beginning, whole-sentence meanings were to take priority over word pronouncing.

What the public didn't know was that Huey never had any experience in teaching reading! According to Samuel Blumenfeld in *Who Killed Excellence?* Huey was merely a puppet for Dewey, James McKeen Cattell, and Edward L. Thorndike. These men were all colleagues at Columbia University. They are the "lethal trio" Professor Blumenfeld considers responsible for wiping out traditional education and killing academic excellence in America. Together they labored "to rebuild American education on a foundation of science, evolution, humanism, and behaviorism. But it was Dewey who identified high literacy as the culprit in traditional education, the sustaining force behind individualism." Dewey also considered early reading a perversion. Therefore, "the attainment of literacy was deliberately de-emphasized in favor of acquiring social skills."

Though the "lethal trio" knew full well that the look-and-say method produced inaccurate readers, they saw to it that *The Psychology and Pedagogy of Reading* was adopted as the "authoritative work" on reading. Huey even argued in favor of inaccuracy as a virtue! Dewey, Cattell, and Thorndike knew that to achieve a collectivist state, they had to change the way children were taught to read.

Today, "look-say permeates the educational marketplace so thoroughly and in so many guises, and it is so widely and uncritically accepted, that it takes expert knowledge by a teacher or parent to know the good from the bad, the useful from the harmful."

Almost all the leaders in the primary reading field began to author basal reading series, for "they had inherited the kingdom of American Education." The rise of the look-and-say approach to reading led to a huge onslaught of basal reading series development. According to Flesch:

> *Look-and-say, after all, was still essentially a gimmick with no scientific foundations whatever. As it had for 150 years, it produced children who couldn't accurately read unfamiliar words. From the fourth grade up, textbooks in all subjects had to be "dumbed down" to accommodate them. Grade promotions had to be based on age rather than achievement. High school diplomas were given to functional illiterates. Colleges had to adjust to an influx of students who couldn't read. The national illiteracy rate climbed year after year after year.*

None of the 124 studies conducted between 1911 and 1981 was able to prove the superiority of look-and-say over phonics. One of the best-known reports is by Dr. Jeanne Chall, Professor of Education at the Harvard Graduate School of Education. Her *Learning to Read: The Great Debate* was the result of three years of intensive research. Dr. Chall reviewed 85 of the studies performed up to the time of the writing of her book. She also conducted laboratory and clinical studies of all kinds to compare results of look-and-say vs. phonics:

*. . . The research from 1912 to 1965 indicates
that a code-emphasis method — i.e., one that views
beginning reading as essentially different from mature reading and emphasizes learning of the printed
code for the spoken language — produces better results, at least up to the point where sufficient evidence seems to be available, the end of third grade.
. . . The results are better, not only in terms of the
mechanical aspects of literacy alone, as was once supposed, but also in terms of the ultimate goals of
reading instruction — comprehension and possibly
even speed of reading.*[21]

In an August 17, 1985, article in *Human Events*, entitled
"Why Are Our Schools Producing Illiterates?" Allan Brownfield
pointed out that "a commission of America's leading reading
specialists issued a U.S. government report entitled 'Becoming a
Nation of Readers,' which argues that there is no good reason
why any child should fail to read. . . . The commission says children should begin with phonics, then move as quickly as possible into stories that use their phonetic knowledge."[22]

There is no good reason why children should fail to read
today. But the philosophers of illiteracy did their jobs well. And
Flesch predicted that, by the 1990's, "we'll join the ranks of
such undereducated Third World countries as the Ivory Coast,
Saudi Arabia, and Zambia. And there'll be few, if any, Nobel
Prize winners who learned to read in an American school."

The Phyllis Schlafly Report, August 1988, said that at least
27 million products of the American public schools are still
illiterate.[23] Another 45 million are unable to read any important book.

Why then does look-and-say still dominate American
schools?

"Could it be that the phonics debate is only a part of a
much broader debate — one concerned with how children are

to be educated and what they are to be taught, rather than merely with whether or not they can read?"

Dr. Chall recognizes that the debate is indeed one of philosophy, not one of "which method gets the best results." "The look-say method," she says, "is associated with 'progressive education' while phonics is associated with 'traditional schooling, with drill and hard work.'" The former opposes a high level of literacy in favor of adapting children to the socialist society. The latter seeks to develop intelligence and skill. And, it prepares the Christian for the service of God.

In "Why Are Our Schools Producing Illiterates?" Mr. Brownfield credits look-and-say dominance to groups like the National Education Association (NEA), who long ago adopted "the progressive ideas of John Dewey, who, quite openly, deprecated widespread literacy as an important goal for the schools." In 1896 Dewey wrote:

> *It is one of the great mistakes of education to make reading and writing constitute the bulk of the school work for the first two years. **The true way is to teach them incidentally as the outgrowth of the social activities at this time.** Thus, language is not primarily the expression of thought, but the means of social communication. . . . It is not claimed that by the method suggested, the child will learn to read as much, nor perhaps as readily in a given period as by the usual method. . . .*(Emphasis added.)

The field of reading research is awash with misinformation and disinformation. "If you select judiciously and avoid interpretations," said Chall, "you can make the research 'prove' almost anything you want it to." She was struck by "how easy it is to misinterpret research findings."

How then can we know the truth? Satan joyfully employs "experts" to lead men astray from God's paths by interpreting statistics and research to adapt to Satan's counterfeits. The

Scriptures provide Christians with our only source for light in this world of darkness!

Consider how being grounded in the Word can affect even the ability to compare phonics with look-and-say:

1. Phonics students learn the mechanics of learning letter/sound combinations first. The phonics method utilizes both "seeing" and "hearing." This enables a student to internalize the characters in a word. God works from the inside/out: "...The LORD looks at the heart [internals]" (1 Sam 16:7b). In contrast, look-and-say students are supposed to learn how to read first by memorizing whole words or whole sentences. Then they may be exposed to the sounds. The look-and-say method relies on "seeing" (sight reading). This keeps the focus on the externals. Man works from the outside/in: ". . . Man looks at the outward appearance [externals] . . ." (1 Sam 16:7b).

2. Phonics students reason through rules, God's order for language, to an accurate conclusion. **Phonics builds faith:** the student taught from a biblical perspective receives phonics/spelling rules in faith. Experience then confirms that faith. In other words, a phonics student walks "into a word" by faith and reasons through to its correct pronunciation or spelling. To spell most words, a phonics student internally hears the sounds and then translates those sounds into written characters or letters by applying rules which govern those sounds. The look-and-say method promotes guessing. This can often lead to an inaccurate conclusion. **Look-and-say builds doubt**: children under the look-and-say method may doubt everything until they experience it, believing "It's true because I proved it." Because a look-and-say student generally has no rules to apply toward a correct pronunciation or spelling, he is at the mercy of his memory. Therefore, many are poor spellers. To spell most words, the look-and-say student must try to recall an external shape of a word from among many that look alike to his mind, for example, *bank* vs. *bark*.

3. **Phonics leads to "liberty"**: using word-attack skills based upon a systematic application of rules produces an unlimited vocabulary. The English language has 26 letters which represent 44 basic sounds. These letter/sound combinations are taught in a specific order, accompanied by basic rules, a reflection of God's orderliness. Once word-attack skills are learned, a world of vocabulary opens for the young reader, which quickly enables him to independently read the Holy Scriptures. **Look-and-say leads to "bondage"**: children are limited in what they can read according to the number of words introduced and remembered. If taught phonics at all, it is usually on a "hit and miss" basis (disorder). Such students are given a controlled vocabulary, which greatly reduces their reading exposure and quality of content. Because of such limitations, the look-and-say student is unable to read the Holy Scriptures early if at all. He's in bondage to words memorized through frequent repetition in dull short stories.

4. One final biblical contrast is that phonics can advance the gospel; look-and-say hinders it. A missionary to an Amazon Indian tribe translated the New Testament into a previously unknown language. He did so by first identifying the sounds which represented ideas in the language of his tribe and then translating those sounds into symbols. After learning the sound/symbol relationships, the Indians could read Scripture for the first time. If that missionary had been limited to the look-and-say, controlled vocabulary method, the Indians would still be without the precious Word of God and in bondage to sin.

Doesn't it make sense that God would provide a simple and orderly method to make His Word available and easy to learn to read? By seeking God's wisdom on this subject, you'll see His hand of blessing upon the development of phonics and that His primary purpose for giving us the alphabet is biblical literacy — to know God and make Him known!

READING READINESS: WHEN SHOULD A CHILD LEARN TO READ?

In our biblical look at reading, we began with its roots in Scripture. Are there also scriptural truths which apply to the subject of reading readiness?

2 Timothy 3:15 says Timothy had known the Scriptures from infancy. He was still young enough to have to be fed, dressed, carried, and watched over. The Greek word translated "known" means that little Timothy had an experiential comprehension of the Scriptures. Even at that tender age, they meant something to him.

Because tiny children still have sensitive hearts, it is common for God to draw them to Himself at very early ages (Matt 19:14). It is not necessary for them to be able to read the Word to be saved (Rom 10:17). However, to grow in the Lord, it is best to combine *hearing* (auditory learning) with *reading* (visual learning). If learning to read is delayed, a vital balance can be lost during the crucial period when the bulk of character, habits, and intellect is being formed.

In his book *Emile*, Rousseau described reading readiness as "the desire to learn."

"What we are in no hurry to get is usually obtained with speed and certainty. I am pretty sure Emile will learn to read and write before he is ten, just because I care very little whether he can do so before he is fifteen. . . ."

Mr. Flesch says learning thrives with strong motivation:

> *If you are willing to wait five or ten years until a child is eager to read, then the teaching of reading will perhaps offer no problem. But our educators, though in theory they are followers of Rousseau, would hardly say out loud that they would postpone the teaching of reading until the age of ten or fifteen. They know very well that people wouldn't stand for it. So, the next best thing, they use any device they*

can to postpone the teaching of reading one, two, three years in the hope that by that time the child will be a little more eager to read.

He went on to say that "Rousseau was wrong when he relied on the necessity to get information. A normal child is ready and eager to learn to read because it's mankind's most fascinating game. . . . Start a child with letters and sounds, make him understand the basic principle underlying all alphabetic writing and reading—and pretty soon he will be on his way, having discovered that reading is fun."

Chall reports that two-thirds of phonics proponents she interviewed believed that most children can benefit from starting as early as five, or even four. One proponent said "the American notion about readiness is absurd. Montessori taught four-year-olds to read." Another said:

> *Reading readiness is vastly overemphasized. I would think that reading readiness is just like talking readiness. We don't investigate too closely whether a child is ready to talk or not. The parents usually encourage the child to talk. They inevitably succeed, although sometimes their child is slower than others.* **In fact, the less anxious the child is to learn to read, the more he should be encouraged to do so, since every child must learn.** (Emphasis added.)

Or, consider this view by James L. Hymes, author of *Teaching Reading to the Under Six Age: A Child Development Point of View:*

> *Teaching reading readiness? Does this mean that the nursery school and kindergarten also teach science readiness? And art readiness? And music readiness? Social studies readiness? Health readiness? The absurdity is self-apparent. The talk of teaching reading readiness as the special approach to the under six age is gobblety gook. We either teach reading or we don't teach reading. . . .*[24]

". . . Linguistic proponents, as a group, called for starting [reading] before age six — at five or even younger," Chall said. "They noted that the five-year-old has a good command of the spoken language. Therefore 'readiness training' should stress learning the letters (in preparation for learning the relation between spoken and written language), rather than practicing oral language, as most of the reading readiness programs now do." Those who "defined beginning reading in terms of learning to decode tended to favor an earlier start and had a more specific conception of readiness. For them, readiness training involved learning to identify and name the letters."

Dr. Chall's comments on reading expert Omar K. Moore's views are enlightening:

> *The best time to start, according to Moore, is at age two or three, . . . when learning is a "game," and when he is not upset by success or failure. The most important readiness factors for Moore are the abilities to sit, speak, and listen to a natural language.*

Moore's success was attributed to the fact that he taught children individually. A one-on-one reading program is by far the best method to develop reading skills. The forced grouping of little children in any school, public or private, works against developing each child according to His own God-given capabilities because some end up being pushed and others held back.

THE ROCKY BAYOU CHRISTIAN SCHOOL STORY

Reading with each kindergartner individually is the major contributor to high reading results at RBCS. Even though RBCS has group instructional periods, classes are kept small. We have a K3 (three-year-old), K4 (four-year-old), and K5 (five-year-old) program. However, within each of those general age groupings are further divisions which allow for more individualized pacing.

All students are evaluated regularly to determine when they're ready to easily begin a reading program. When that time occurs, each child will read with a teacher on a one-on-one basis with parents conducting brief reading practices in the home. None are pushed to achieve beyond individual abilities nor are any held back. No pressure is ever applied to make one child perform like another. That violates good teaching methods as well as God's law of love. Year after year, for the past 21 years, I have seen RBCS kindergartners learn to read with ease. In fact, it is common by the end of the five-year-old program to be able to quickly locate and read any passage in Scripture well. As for whether or not the early start lasts, our experience has been that children who have gone through the kindergarten program are by far the best students throughout their school years.

How did this come about? In my early years at RBCS, I hadn't heard much about the different views on reading readiness. Therefore, I simply started by teaching letters and sounds. I also bathed the teaching process in prayer. Through the children themselves, more and more of their capabilities unfolded. The pacing rate for reading instruction was established by their own God-given capabilities. In the process, I discovered that phonics, spelling, and writing was indeed like a fascinating game to the children. Not until a 1981 administrators' conference did I learn that some educators felt little children shouldn't read until they first became socially and physically "ready." Professor Diane Ravitch disagreed.

> *A . . . myth that has been dispatched is that children should not be taught to read until socially and physically "ready." Getting ready meant learning how to skip, to hop, and to cut with scissors. Believing this, many teachers discouraged children from reading "too soon." Research now shows that skipping, hopping, and using scissors are not related to*

reading skills. Children learn to read by direct experience with oral and written language.

Until that administrators' conference I also had never heard the belief that early reading can cause myopia (nearsightedness). Not wanting to create problems out of ignorance, I went to the Lord. He led me to write to Dr. Melvin Rubin, Chairman of the Ophthalmology Department at the University of Florida College of Medicine in Gainesville, Florida (and currently president of the American Association of Ophthalmologists).

On April 2, 1981, Dr. Rubin responded by phone. He reassured me that teaching children to read early was not going to damage their eyes and that "the amount of time the eyes are used makes no difference."

"Teach them to read," he said, "the earlier the better! The sooner children can read, the better, because they will continue to be more advanced all the way through life."

On August 8, 1988, I contacted Dr. Rubin again. Were there any new findings in eye research to indicate that early reading should now be avoided?

Dr. Rubin indicated that one of the reasons for any controversy at all in this area is that laymen often confuse regular myopia with progressive myopia. He explained that "progressive myopia is not induced by reading. Regular myopia and the progressive form just aren't the same thing." Then he went on to say, "Maybe reading does increase chances of regular myopia, but if it does, so what? Even at the maximum amount, it's no more than a diopter or so. It just isn't significant. Regular myopia isn't sign of a disease, but sign of growth, which is insignificant.

"It's never too early to teach a child to read," he said. "If he can read at age one, God bless him, teach him to read! If a child is ready to read, he'll read. If not ready, don't frustrate him." To reassure me, he suggested I talk with two pediatric ophthalmologists whom he considers "world class."

The first was Dr. Paul Romano, one of Dr. Rubin's associates at the University of Florida College of Medicine. I spoke with him on August 9th. When asked about whether early reading can damage the eyes, he replied, "What do you mean by damage? To me, 'damage' is included under the heading of something which would cause loss of maximum function such as to prevent 20/20 vision even with glasses. The problem with early reading, if it really is a problem, is myopia or nearsightedness which is not 'damage' but is accelerated growth change. Perhaps there's some evidence that reading does exaggerate changes in the eye. The earlier it's detected, however, the better the chances to correct it. There are treatments on the horizon which suggest medically this can be offset."

He went on to explain, "With normal eye growth during school years, children tend to get nearsighted. There may be some growth change in the eyes, but not organic damage. In other words, a child may need glasses to see clearly, to have 20/20 vision. Possibly, if you start earlier, there is a tendency with excessive reading to exaggerate the growth of the eyes, but that's a very small price to pay. Even if you wait until age six, that doesn't stop this potential problem. There are bonafide cases of students who got along very well until graduate school. Once there, they get to be serious as students and at that point start to be nearsighted. This is especially true of law students who do intensive amounts of reading. Once they hit the books for three to four years, by 25 years of age, they'll develop progressive nearsightedness."

I asked Dr. Romano if he had any recommendations concerning how long a child could safely read at one sitting. "There's no way to say how long, because there are simply too many variables," he said. "For example, there can be two 'A' students — one who has glasses that look like the bottom of old coke bottles, and the other who's just fine. A certain number of people who are genetically disposed can develop nearsightedness from a lot of reading. However, we have no right to call it damage unless it's severe. There never has been a link made between very bad myopia (pathological) and reading. To the best of my knowledge, there's never been a hook-up between pathological myopia, i.e., 'damage,' and the use of the eyes. Myopia is inherited, like diabetes."

As for precautions for those who may be genetically disposed to develop myopia, Dr. Romano said, "We're now working on screening children from early ages on to catch them when they first start to get nearsighted. For most children, there is a leeway of one to two years when you can see it coming if you measure the state of the eyes at frequent intervals. Ideally, every child should be screened at six months of age by an ophthalmologist, preferably a pediatric ophthalmologist. This will give an idea if optically there is a likelihood of becoming nearsighted. Then, when you start to teach a child to read, say around age three, have him checked again. Once you start, then have an exam once a year to find out what's happening. If you catch it early you can work to offset it — or use other treatments which may be recommended in the future."

If both parents are myopic, Dr. Romano said that there is probably a 100% probability their children will be too. Those parents, especially, should have their children under the care of a pediatric ophthalmologist from early on, he said.

"There's no medical reason to say a child should not be able to read or not encouraged to read at an early age," Romano said. "A far greater handicap is to hamper a child's intellectual development, because that will stay with him the rest of his life. It's far better to take the risk a child may be a little more nearsighted and have to wear glasses than to hamper him intellectually."

108

On August 9th, I talked with Dr. George Beauchamp, another pediatric ophthalmologist. He is associated with the Cleveland Clinic and serves as president of the National Children's Eye Care Foundation. "Does early reading cause myopia or in any other way damage the eyes?" I asked.

"There just isn't any good science to back up that it does," he said. "On the one hand, there are certainly youngsters that read like bandits since age two and never see myopia. Yet in others, we find that they're more susceptible. But the data is just not there to draw hard and fast conclusions."

After reading Dr. Rubin's earlier statement about laymen confusing regular myopia with the progressive form, and that even at a maximum amount any eye changes as result of reading were insignificant, he commented, "I would certainly agree with that! Don't try to hold children back from reading early!"

One other warning was presented at that 1981 administrators' conference. We were told that reading too early could cause irreparable damage — socially, mentally, and physically.

Since these areas have already been addressed one way or another, I'll just mention Flesch's contrasting viewpoint that delaying reading can cause "irreparable damage." He reasons that the "majority of our children are unable to read Andersen's *Fairy Tales* and *The Arabian Nights* and Mark Twain and Louisa May Alcott and Robert Louis Stevenson and Edgar Allen Poe and Charles Dickens and Conan Doyle **at the age when they would truly enjoy those books**." (Emphasis added.)

> *In England, where the relationship between age and reading ability is normal and undistorted, five-year-olds are able to read nursery tales. They are able to read material that is natural for their age. . . . When children are mentally ready for fairy tales, they can read fairy tales; when they are ready for Sir Walter Scott, they can read Scott; when they are ready for Dickens, they can read Dickens.*

When Dr. Chall visited in English infant-schools, she found that five-year-olds were expected to read. When she pointed out to one of their principals that in America our educators are upset about the growing trend toward formal reading instruction in kindergarten, the principal couldn't understand why.

"Five-year-olds enjoy a little work," the principal said. "We would not know what to do with them the entire school day if they could not do a little reading. They get tired of playing. They want to work and do a little reading." Yet, in our country, there's the feeling that "reading instruction at age five will strain the child." In both England and America, Chall said she has often heard "the long refuted belief: 'Well, as you know, research says that a mental age of six or six-and-a-half is best for starting.'"

After comparing 59 studies of look-and-say vs. phonics, Dr. Robert Dykstra, professor of education at the University of Minnesota, found:

> We can summarize the results of 60 years of research dealing with beginning reading instruction by stating that **early systematic instruction in phonics provides the child with the skills necessary to become an independent reader at an earlier age than is likely if phonics is delayed or less systematic**. As a consequence of his early success in "learning to read," the child can more quickly go about the job of "reading to learn." (Emphasis added.)

In a rather humorous note, Flesch comments:

> After all the research that has been done in the past twenty years on preschool and kindergarten reading, you may doubt that the now-antique concept of "reading readiness" is still alive and kicking. It most certainly is. At the slightest provocation it's

being taken out of mothballs and thrown in the face
of the poor mother who doesn't know any better. The
history of so-called reading readiness is, if possible,
even funnier than the other Mickey Mouse research
I've met on my safari through deepest Educatoria.

When bombarded with information from "experts," how can we discern the truth? Just as God expects us to be good Bereans by checking out what is heard from the pulpit concerning His special revelation, so He holds us responsible to check out what we're told about His natural revelation. To help you more effectively do that when it comes to evaluating research and statistics, here are a few tips:

First, do not automatically disregard research and statistics. For example, I do not assert that humanistic atheists like Dewey, Skinner, Fletcher and others say nothing that is correct. Certainly, what they say about God is not correct, nor is their basic concept of man. In fact, when they are speaking from their presuppositions rather than simply reporting scientific data they are very likely to be wrong because their basic presuppositions are wrong.

There is a big difference between a secular humanistic world view and a biblical world view. Their presuppositions are antithetical concerning such major elements as the nature of God, the nature of man, the purpose of man and the concepts of salvation, ethics, and authority. When a humanist reports scientific data or interprets it in a way that does not conflict with God's Word, however, he may very well be saying something that is correct.

Secondly, to evaluate truth in the normative aspect you need to use biblical standards or criteria. To evaluate truth in the strictly positive or scientific aspect, try to ensure the scientific method is being used correctly and that studies purporting to be scientific are not merely pseudo-scientific attempts to support preconceived notions of reality. Regardless of who it is, their work should be subjected to the critical process inherent in the free marketplace of ideas, and Christians are obligated to meet the same standards of science applicable to anyone else. God's Word and scientific accuracy are the tests of truth. True science will always be consistent with God's Word.

Keeping your eyes on Christ will help you be alert to the behind-the-scenes dramas of the heavens. The Holy Spirit longs to teach you His biblical world view so that our focus is not on this temporary world but the eternal one (2 Cor 4:18).

Our sovereign Lord has promised: "I will destroy the wisdom of the wise; the intelligence of the intelligent I will frustrate. Where is the wise man? Where is the scholar? Where is the philosopher of this age? Has not God made foolish the wisdom of this world?" (1 Cor 1:19-20, NIV).

Faith should not rest on men's wisdom, but on God's power (1 Cor 2:5) and in His wisdom (James 1:5). Regardless of educational background, therefore, the Lord can and will lead you into His truth.

But reading is just the beginning. It is God's desire that His children reclaim the other disciplines as well.

Chapter Five

Delighting in God Through Other Subjects

※※

"The works of the Lord are great, Studied by all who have pleasure in them. His work is honorable and glorious, And His righteousness endures forever. He hath made his wonderful works to be remembered; The Lord is gracious and full of compassion" (Psa 111:2-4).

GOD IN MATH

Math reflects God's glory, because math is rooted in God's very nature. The nature of all things is dependent upon God. The nature of God, His unity in plurality, is the basis for mathematics. To properly understand math, we need to consider how God's unity/plurality governs mathematical truth.

The key to understanding the unity of all things is seen in Jesus Christ Himself. He holds all things together: "For by Him all things were created that are in heaven and that are on earth, visible and invisible, whether thrones or dominions or principalities or powers. All things were created through Him and for Him. And He is before all things, and in Him all things consist" (Col 1:16-17).

We can study all things from a biblical perspective, because all things are obedient to God's law. Without His law, there is no unity. Unity is based upon God's sovereignty. It is He who says what shall be true for His creation. Unless you understand that God is totally in control, you are left with nothing but chance to explain the world. Evolution is based upon the idea that chance is preeminent. Unity is seen in the fact that all things are obedient to the will of God, which is His law. And this gives us the Source for the absoluteness of mathematical truth.

To understand math, we must also understand God's plurality, that is, His trinitarian nature. "Plurality" literally means "consisting of two or more of the same kind." In God's triune nature we see that He is truly one God, one essence or being. Yet He exists in three Persons. Though He is One, He is also three (1 John 5:7).

We can relate this plurality to the word "diversity," meaning "there's a difference, or variety." When we have diversity, we immediately set up numbers. Numbers are simply the recognition of differences. For example, when we teach a little child to start counting, "1, 2, 3, 4, and so on," what we're actually doing is teaching him that there is plurality, or diversity in God's creation. That's where numbers come from.

Without the unity and plurality in our triune God's nature, there is no true math. In other words, you have no basis to be able to talk about individual phenomena, individual numbers, because you have no way to relate them in integral or complete wholeness to each other. There's no way to have a system.

Mathematical operations are an important part of God's system. For example, God made a day and he divided it into evening and morning. He made one day, then He added something to it. He commanded animals to multiply upon the earth, adding numbers of "like things" (plurality) to His creation. He subtracted a rib from Adam, then He added another human, Eve.

Diversity enables us to add one tree to another tree and determine it makes two trees. In that simple addition problem, we see plurality ("adding the same kind") and unity ("one tree plus one tree always equals two trees"). God's law requires that it be so.

Mathematically, addition is the basis of all other operations. So we start there. The first thing God did was to add something to the nothing that existed, "the heavens and the earth (Gen 1:1)." His first act was one of addition. Addition is generally used in connection with adding blessings, usually a result of obedience. However, sometimes the term "add" has an undesirable connotation such as when God "adds" a curse as a result of disobedience. Addition and subtraction are operational inverses. Inverse means "reverse order." In other words, it is a "doing/undoing" relationship.

Addition is related to multiplication in that multiplication is simply a quick way to do addition. For example, when we say "3 x 5," all we're saying is "3 added together 5 times" or "5 added together 3 times." Multiplication is based upon addition. Therefore, scripturally speaking, it too is viewed in terms of blessings. An example of this is God's command to "be fruitful and multiply" to fill the earth. God multiplied His creation in the initial six-day period. Now we are commanded to imitate what He has done, in obedience to His law of replenishing His kingdom and exercising dominion over it.

Division is related to multiplication in the same way subtraction is to addition. In division, you unmultiply. In other words, you split up what has been multiplied. Division implies a result. For example, God's division of mankind at the tower of Babel was a result of disobedience to His law. (A profitable exercise would be to take a concordance and look up all the instances of God's exercising His mathematical laws in the basic operations.)

Mathematics, then, demonstrates that God has given law with blessings and curses. Addition and multiplication are generally related to blessings as a result of obedience; subtraction and division are often related to curses as a result of disobedience. Our great God uses things we understand as lessons to describe His nature.

The study of biblical numerology is an example of object lessons which teach truths about His nature. For instance, there is a general consensus that "one" is "God's number." In Zechariah 14:9 we learn that His name is "one." The number "one" means that there is "no other"; there is "no other" God. Or, consider the number 10, which is more or less a divine basis for our number system. One of the key factors for this is the decalogue, the ten commandments, which was the encapsulation of the law God gave His people at Mount Sinai. In Scripture, there appears to be enough evidence that warrants viewing 10 as the number representing completeness of divine order. Therefore, it seems logical that 10 would represent a completeness of God's number cycle as well. Studying the biblical meaning of these and other numbers can be very exciting!

We can also see God in the mathematical notion of *place*. Just as God designed a dwelling place for Himself, the tabernacle, so He designed a dwelling place for numbers. The mathematical notion of place is the understanding that numbers make sense only in their notational context. In other words, just as a string of words in language means nothing without grammar and syntax, so place value determines the meaning of numbers in notation. This is the "decently and in order" principle which is the key to the placement of numbers in their meaningful context. Furthermore, in place value, you have the recognition of the cyclical nature of numbers in the cycles of the moon, year, and seasons — all God-ordained according to His law. From the position of convenience, as well as reflecting order in the universe, we need to realize that numbers do occur in patterns and cycles.

God's nature is also revealed through the patterns and cycles of fractions, time, and money. Fractions are essentially division problems. Fractions take a whole and divide it into parts, whether it's one pie divided into eight pieces or one apple divided into halves. This simply reflects that wholes are made up of parts. This is reflective of God's unity/plurality — three Persons in one God. From the tiniest created thing to the grandest, we find so many parts to the whole that man can't enumerate them all!

That aspect of God's creation which we call *time*, we also enumerate. We divide it into parts of the whole. Time is created by God with a beginning and an ending. However, God does not reside in time, which is the passage of one moment to the next, measuring the duration of actions. Time deals with God's plan for the universe. He works all things after the counsel of His own will (Eph 1:11). Measurement and passage of time are constant reminders that man is not autonomous. God appoints the time of our birth and time of our death (Heb 9:27). We cannot escape time. God expects us to look at its patterns and use it His way and for His glory! Like the Psalmist, we should exclaim, "What is man that You are mindful of him. . .? As for man, his days are like grass; as a flower of the field, so he flourishes" (Psa 8:4, 103:15).

Money is another part of God's creation which we enumerate. Money is simply an application of quantity and quality to the things God has made. It is related to weight and measures which are the numerical qualities of physical objects. In the Scriptures, money is derived from the weight of a valuable substance. Silver, gold, and copper are the metals valued highly enough to be used as coinage. The whole point of a coin is that it is the value of that weight of that particular precious metal. Money is necessary to the functioning of a commercial economy (viz., the accepted value of different animals as sacrifices in Levitical Law). Gold and silver are seen as being created by God for use as money. Our modern notion of money being backed by the state is not found in Scripture. Correct use of money is one aspect of exercising dominion for Christ.

Everything in God's creation has numerical quality, its little mathematical tab. Applying mathematical principles and operations practically in God's universe helps to fulfill His commandment to use all things lawfully. Solving word problems by taking the tools of math and applying them to practical situations is a major way of accomplishing that objective. Such an understanding is required for the exercise of wise stewardship over the resources God has given. If children have nothing but math facts in their heads and don't learn to apply these in a godly way for godly purposes, their knowledge is useless.

Math is truth, because God made it that way. It is something you can always rely on. Enjoy the concreteness of math, and pass that joy on to your children! God's creation is so reflective of His grandeur that it ought to bring us all to our knees shouting: "You, LORD, have made me glad through Your work; I will triumph in the works of Your hands. O LORD, how great are Your works! Your thoughts are very deep" (Psa 92:4-5).

GOD IN HISTORY

Just as math has its roots in God's sovereignty, so does history. Humanistic man views history as being cyclical, that is, it repeats itself. The biblical perspective is that history is linear. Time is simply one segment of God's sovereign plan.

God existed before man. History is therefore "His story"; it is not the story of man. Thus, the beginning of history is not the Garden of Eden, because Jesus Christ, our Creator, existed before history as we know it (Psa 90:2, Prov 8:23 and 25-26, John 1:1-3, Psa 148:2-5). Christ is the focal point of all history.

A biblical perspective of history, therefore, begins with God, who is the Spirit (John 4:24), life (John 5:26), self-existent (Ex 3:14), infinite (Psa 145:3), immutable or changeless (Psa 102:27, James 1:17), truth (Deut 32:4, John 17:3), love (1 John 4:8), eternal (Psa 90:2), holy (1 Pet 1:16), omnipresent (Psa 139:8), omniscient (Psa 147:4-5), and omnipotent (Matt 19:26). God is sovereign over His creation (Psa 103:19-22, Matt 28:18). No aspect of His creation is too large for Him to completely control. And no detail, even to the falling of a sparrow, is too small to be included in His sovereign plan (Eph 1:11). While the Bible applies several names to God, the name He gives to Himself is Jehovah, which emphasizes self-existence (Ex 3:13-14). He is our Creator, Savior, and Lord!

God Himself "has made from one blood every nation of men to dwell on all the face of the earth, and has determined their preappointed times and the boundaries of their dwellings . . . for in Him we live and move and have our being" (Acts 17:26, 28a). In light of who He is, we are responsible to yield ourselves to Him, to be instruments in His hands for the carrying out of His perfect plan (Rom 12:1-2). History records how He carries out His purposes. He has not left us in the dark concerning how to interpret historical records. In Scripture, we're told that "all these things happened to them [past generations] as examples, and they were written for our admonition, upon whom the ends of the ages have come (1 Cor 10:11). For whatever things were written before were written for our learning, that we through the patience and comfort of the Scriptures might have hope" (Rom 15:4). Paul Jehle writes:

> *The lessons from history . . . demonstrate the character that was needed to forge new ideas, as well as teaching us good models to emulate, and failures that we should not repeat. Often, our view of the past becomes our view of the future, and gives us a perspective of where we are at present. It is important*

> *. . . to show that, by principle, God is teaching His*
> *people through history (His story) to have Hope.*[25]

Historical records, therefore, are not simply a collection of facts and dates. Rather history is intended to serve as both a national and a personal warning and admonition to live according to holiness. The success or failure of nations, however, begins with the individual:

> He knows not how to rule a kingdom,
>
> that cannot manage a Province;
>
> Nor can he wield a Province, that cannot order a City;
>
> Nor can he order a City;
>
> that knows not how to regulate a Village;
>
> Nor he a Village, that cannot guide a Family;
>
> Nor can that man Govern well a Family,
>
> that knows not how to Govern himself;
>
> Neither can any Govern himself
>
> unless his reason be Lord, Will and Appetite her Vassals:
>
> Nor can Reason rule unless herself be ruled by God,
>
> and wholly be obedient to Him.
>
> —Hugh Grotius, 1654

To be wholly obedient to God requires Christian self-government. The greatest historical models to emulate have been from those periods in which self-governing Christians were willing to obey God at any cost. What are the characteristics of a self-governing Christian? Author Rose Weiner aptly explains:

> *A self-governing Christian labors with God; he does not labor without God or against God. A self-governing person acts from internal convictions, acting because a thing is right. Self-government is rooted in self-control. Self-control is the ability to order one's life according to what one senses God wants one to do, or according to what God commands in His*

Word. A person who is not self-governed is a person whose life is ordered by whims, moods, and essentially whatever he "feels" like doing.[26]

Because we've lost our Christian heritage, the "if it feels good, do it" mentality prevails even in the lives of many Christians. The greatest need we all have is to acquire "the ability to order one's life according to what one senses God wants one to do, or according to what God commands in His Word," for strong Christian self-government, or the lack of it, affects all other forms of government (family, church, civil, vocational, and economic).

The best foundation we can provide for our children is one which stresses the importance of recognizing God's plan for man — to glorify God and enjoy Him forever. We can glorify God only to the degree that we exercise Christian self-government through the power of the Holy Spirit. We can learn of God's sovereign plan for us in the Holy Scriptures as well as in a study of history.

For example, not only does God preappoint each nation's times and boundaries, but He also controls each nation's actions, using them to fulfill His purposes. *"By me kings reign, And rulers decree justice. By me princes rule, and nobles, All the judges of the earth" (Prov 8:15-16).*

In another passage God tells us that "the king's heart is in the hand of the LORD, Like the rivers of water; He turns it wherever He wishes (Prov 21:1)." We see this even in His use of heathen nations to inflict His judgment upon rebellious Israel (e.g., Judges 2:14-15; 2 Kings 17:6-18; Jer 46:24-26). Yet, those nations who are instruments of His judgment are still held accountable for their iniquity (e.g., Isa 10:12-15; Jer 25:11-12; Zech 1:12-15). We could therefore say that a nation's whole history depends upon its relationship to God and His people (see Jonah 3:5-10; Joel 3:1-8, 12, 19; Matt 25:32-46). Or, as Oliver Cromwell once said, "What are all histories but

God manifesting himself, shaking down and trampling under foot whatsoever he hath not planted."

When history is viewed from that simple perspective, it makes all the difference in the world. It brings meaning to the rise and fall of empires, to the times of victories and the times of suffering and anguish men have endured. And, it brings hope for those who are grounded in the Rock, Jesus Christ, in the midst of a world of seeming chaos. For we know that the final victory is already won in Him. The making of history is like being on a ship headed for a particular destination. Passengers on that ship have freedom to make daily decisions, yet within certain limitations. Each is responsible for his actions which can merit favorable or unfavorable consequences. However, the Pilot of the ship will see to it that all passengers reach His ordained port.

Ultimately, all the ends of the earth will turn to the LORD. All families of the nations shall worship before Him (Psa 22:27). "For the kingdom is the LORD's, And He rules over the nations" (Psa 22:28). "Yes, all kings shall fall down before Him; All nations shall serve Him" (Psa 72:11). We know that at the name of Jesus every knee will bow and that every tongue will confess that Jesus Christ is Lord, to the glory of God the Father (Phil 2:10-11)!

"Who shall not fear You, O Lord, and glorify Your name? For You alone are holy. For all nations shall come and worship before You, For Your judgments have been manifested" (Rev 15:4).

This is history: the manifestations of God's judgments.

GOD IN SCIENCE

According to *The Christian World View of Science and Technology*, science, "man's attempt to observe, understand, and explain the operation of the universe and its inhabitants," is a response to God's command to subdue the earth and exercise dominion over His creation (Gen 1:28).

Technology is "the use of the knowledge gained by scientific research for mankind's practical benefit, bringing portions of the universe under his control." [27]

In order to properly understand God's workmanship, science and technology must be brought under the authority of Jesus Christ, the sovereign Creator (John 1:1-3). God's Word is absolute truth and provides the basis for scientific truth (John 17:17). Therefore, true science will always be consistent with the Scriptures.

The world, created in six solar days, was created for God's purpose and pleasure (Col 1:16, Rev 4:11). All of creation was meant to praise God and give Him glory (Psa 103:20-22; Psa 111:2, 4; Psa 148:2-13; Psa 150:6; Rom 11:36). God is the Sustainer of the universe. The universe functions according to His plan (Neh 9:6, Psa 119:90-91, Col 1:17, Heb 1:3), for His world is a world of order (Gen 1:14; Gen 8:22; Eccl 1:4-7; Eccl 3:11; Job 38:31-33; Amos 5:8).

Everything God created in the beginning was perfect (Gen 1), even man, who was created in the image of God (Gen 1:27). When Adam disobeyed God, sin entered the world. As a result, the earth was cursed, and man was in need of a Savior (Gen 3:17-19; Rom 5:12). The whole creation groans to be delivered from the bondage of corruption (Rom 8:20-22).

Because of the Fall, most men knowingly choose to deny God's revelation of the biblical origin and operation of the universe. As a result of sin, according to Rushdoony, "science in the modern world has for many replaced God as the source of authority." The tendency now is to falsely "believe that science, rather than Scripture, is the primary source of truth." The Christian, however, is commanded to avoid "the profane and idle babble and contradictions of what is falsely called knowledge (1 Tim 6:20)." We should instead actively pursue a biblical view of science and technology.

Even though man can never fully understand creation (Eccl 3:11; Isa 55:9; Rom 11:33-34), God expects us to study His natural revelation so we can exercise wise stewardship over it (Gen 1:28; Job 12:7-8). This can be a challenge, because creation is in a constant state of change (Job 14:7-9, 19; Isa 24:4, 40:7, 51:6; Matt 6:19). Yet, God Himself never changes (Heb 1:10-12). In Christ are "hidden all treasures of wisdom and knowledge" (Col 2:3). Because His thoughts are not our thoughts nor His ways our ways (Isa 55:8), He speaks to us in terms we can understand.

In some cases, God uses object lessons from nature to teach us about His truths. For example, the rainbow serves as a constant reminder that He'll never flood the whole earth again (Gen 9:13-17). God miraculously lengthened one day to grant Israel's prayers for victory (Josh 10:13-14). In Job 38-41; 42:16, our sovereign God used creation to teach Job a lesson about His omnipotence. (Consider also Psa 8:3-4; Isa 55:9-11; Matt 5:44-45, 6:25-34; Rom 1:20; Heb 3:3-4.)

Even little children get excited about what they learn from God's creation. Imagine your reaction if your five-year-old came bouncing into the room and announced, "Momma, if the orbit of a comet is open it goes off into outer space never to be seen again! If the orbit is closed it may be expected to return!"

Most likely, such a comment would floor you a little, as it did Carla Alldredge when her five-year-old son said just that. Astounded, she exclaimed, "Hey, Josiah, that's pretty good! Where did you learn that?"

He nonchalantly responded, "Oh, from one of Daddy's astronomy books." That evening, Josiah shared the same information with his father, then concluded, "The only problem I have, Daddy, is that I don't know what an orbit is!" Brian, a science teacher at Rocky Bayou Christian School, delightedly captured a teaching opportunity.

Already an avid reader, Josiah reads the Word himself (usually when he goes down for a nap). In addition, learning four verses a week is routine for him.

"As parents," Carla says, "we struggle to memorize Scripture but Josiah just soaks it up — and the verses stay with him. Though he sometimes forgets the references, memorized passages regularly come to mind when he sees circumstances which fit the verses."

Josiah is being trained to use his growing knowledge of Scripture to spot false thinking in the science books he reads. When finding something false, he enjoys showing it to his parents. Carla says she often hears him laugh loudly as he calls out, "Momma! They've got this all wrong! That's not what happened! God created the world! I want to learn about real things — not evolution!"

Carla and Brian are heeding God's warning against exposing little ones to anything which could undermine their faith (Matt 18:6). Even at age five, Josiah is being trained how to not just accept so-called scientific evidence, which may be tainted with preconceived philosophical biases. For science divorced from God is pseudo-science, "science falsely so called (1 Tim 6:20, KJV)."

From the beginning, therefore, we should teach children that the practical aspects of science are to be used to exercise dominion for Jesus Christ through good stewardship (Luke 16:1-13). The ultimate attitude toward the revelation of God's creation should be continual praise:

> *"PRAISE the Lord! Praise the Lord from the heavens; Praise Him in the heights! Praise Him, all His angels; Praise Him, all His hosts! Praise Him, sun and moon; Praise Him, all you stars of light! Praise Him, you heavens of heavens, And you waters above the heavens! Let them praise the name of the Lord, For He commanded and they were created" (Psa 148:1-5).*

"Let everything that has breath praise the LORD. Praise the LORD!" (Psa 150:6).

GOD IN ART

Christian art can be one of the highest forms of giving praise to God. Since Christ has all authority (Matt 28:18), Christian art needs to be brought under His sovereign lordship. It should, therefore, reflect God's attributes and be designed for His honor and glory.

God's creativity always begins with order. Two examples of this are the instructions He gave Noah for the building of the ark and Moses for the tabernacle and worship. Man "creates" with what Christ has already created, for "there is nothing new under the sun" (Eccl 1:9).

For instance, suppose an art lesson is drawing/coloring an illustration of apples. A child has a legitimate creative choice of creativity within God's pattern for order. One child might choose to color the apples green. Another may decide his are red. A student who has a greater eye for detail might draw several apples shaded with green and yellow or red. The size, shape, position on the paper, and number of apples drawn are also proper choices which allow a child the opportunity to demonstrate his own unique creativity.

Suppose, however, that an apple was pictured the shape of a banana and colored purple or drawn the size of a grape and colored black. Would those choices follow God's order for art?

Although a young child would not consciously be sinning, sin is at the root of man's artistic choices that run contrary to God's order of design. In Exodus 32:1-4, God records rebellion against Himself when the people created the golden calf as a replacement for Almighty Jehovah. God's Word teaches that creativity needs spiritual guidance.

"Then the LORD spoke to Moses saying: 'See, I have called by name Bezaleel the son of Uri, the son of Hur, of the tribe of Judah. And I have filled him with the Spirit of God, in wisdom, in understanding, in knowledge, and in all kinds of workmanship, to design artistic works, to work in gold, in silver, in bronze, in cutting jewels for setting, in carving wood, and to work in all kinds of workmanship'" (Ex 31:1-5).

Bezaleel had a special God-given ability, as may one of your children. Most children, however, are just average art students whose ability can be enhanced through spiritual guidance and technical training. A few will never be able to perform well in art but can at least be taught to recognize the beauty in God's creation so that they can genuinely appreciate the diversity of gifts He's given to others. Regardless of the level of ability, each is responsible to yield that ability to God's direction and for His glory.

Under God's direction, a Christian's artwork will not only reflect God's orderliness but also reflect His attention to detail. Numbering the hairs on our heads (Matt 10:30) is an example. In fact, everything that He has created is so complex that it can not be seen entirely with the human eye. Yet, the more we see of God's creation, the more we come to know Him. We reveal this knowledge to others when we capture the detail of His creation in art.

Some would say that children can express themselves artistically only according to their age group. Such educators believe the most which can be expected of young children is lollipop figures, which is as if to say that when a child looks at a tree he does not see the same thing that an adult would see.

A child who is able to believe in God is also able to see His creation as an adult sees it.

God reveals Himself through His creation. If a child were incapable of fully perceiving it, he could not be held accountable for his unbelief as referred to in Romans 1:20:

"For since the creation of the world His invisible attributes are clearly seen, being understood by the things that are made, even His eternal power and Godhead, so that they are without excuse. . . ."

Art has order — *lines*, *shapes*, *values*, *colors*, and *textures*. And we need to see how that order relates to God.

First, let's consider *line/shape*. When a little child scribbles, secular educators tell us, "He's expressing himself." In reality, scribbling is only line without order. For example, when a child is taught to write, we teach him to control the line so it makes a specific letter. It is the same process in teaching shapes such as a circle, triangle, or square. These are called the three basic shapes. Sometimes we speak about these shapes in relationship to God. The circle represents God as having no beginning or ending, the triangle speaks of the Trinity, and the square says God is everywhere, even to the four corners of the earth.

Next in the order of art is *value*. Value is the lightness or darkness of an object such as the earth in Genesis 1:2-3:

"The earth was without form, and void; and darkness was on the face of the deep. And the Spirit of God was hovering over the face of the waters. Then God said, 'Let there be light'; and there was light."

It is through the light that we see God's beauty:

"The lamp of the body is the eye. If therefore your eye is good, your whole body will be full of light" (Matt 6:22).

The more light the greater the value:

". . . God is light and in Him is no darkness at all" (1 John 1:5).

Without light, there is no *color*. The brighter the light the more brilliant the colors. Picture the new Jerusalem where God is the light:

> *"The city had no need of the sun or of the moon*
> *to shine in it, for the glory of God illuminated it.*
> *The Lamb is its light" (Rev 21:23).*

God's order for color can be found in the rainbow, which is the true spectrum for color. The raindrops act as a prism through which light passes creating the colors. In the rainbow there are seven colors. Seven is God's number of spiritual perfection or completion. The colors are red, orange, yellow, green, blue, purple, and indigo. Red, yellow, and blue are known as primary colors. Orange, green, and purple are secondary colors, since they are derived from the primary colors. Indigo, which is blue-violet, seems to be a totally independent color which cannot be seen with the naked eye.

The fourth element in the order of art is *texture*. Through texture we can feel the uniqueness of God's creation. We learn that objects are not flat, but that each thing has a different shape and feel. For instance, you might ask a child to hold an apple in his hand to feel its shape before he draws it. Upon examination, he should conclude that it looks and feels round like a ball. Its basic shape is therefore a circle. Applying the principle of basic shapes to art can quickly enhance a little child's artistic development.

From their earliest years, we should seek to instill in our children a desire to develop creativity with excellence: "And whatever you do, do it heartily, as to the Lord and not to men" (Col 3:23). Artistic ability which is yielded to the Lord glorifies God.

May this be the artist's prayer:

> *"And let the beauty of the Lord our God be*
> *upon us, And establish the work of our hands for us;*
> *Yes, establish the work of our hands" (Psa 90:17).*

If a child has no artistic ability, he needs to understand that he is God's handiwork created in Christ Jesus for good works (Eph 2:10). Even the greatest artistic masterpiece can never compare to God's workmanship of a life wholly consecrated to Him. Francis Schaeffer well states:

> No work of art is more important than the Christian's own life, and every Christian is called upon to be an artist in this sense. He may have no gift of creativity in terms of the way he lives his life. In this sense, the Christian life is to be a thing of truth and also a thing of beauty in the midst of a lost and despairing world.[28]

GOD IN MUSIC

Music is of God. It has existed for as long as God has existed. Music is common even in heaven (e.g., Ezek 28:13; 1 Cor 15:52; Heb 2: 9-12; Rev 5:8-9, 14:2-3, 15:2-3). When God created the heavens and the earth, the morning stars sang together and all the sons of God shouted for joy (Job 38:7)! All of creation sings praises to God's name (1 Chron 16:23, 33; Psa 65:13, 104:12; Sol 2:12; Isa 44:23)!

The Scriptures indicate that God Himself sings:

> "The Lord your God in your midst, The Mighty One, will save; He will rejoice over you with gladness, He will quiet you with His love, He will rejoice over you with singing" (Zeph 3:17).

Even though the Hebrew word (*rinnah*) translated "singing" in the King James Version has a primary meaning of "shout," "singing" is one of the alternate translations. According to Leonard J. Seidel:

> There are perhaps more references to music in the Bible than to any other subject. From the mention of Jubal as the inventor of instruments in Genesis 4:21 to the great choruses of heaven mentioned in The Revelation, God's Word is rich with instruction in

principles, requirements, qualifications, ensembles, in-
struments and general musical knowledge.[29]

Throughout Scripture, music is used to praise and worship Almighty God. It also refreshes God's people as we sing praises together to the Lord. When His Word dwells in us richly, a natural response is an outburst of musical praise. Through Psalms (Scripture set to music), hymns (adoration to, or of God) and spiritual songs (songs of response to the Word of God), the lost can also be led to repentance.

In his *Bible Handbook*, Henry Halley says congregational singing, next to Bible teaching, is the best feature of a religious service, the most effective way to preach the gospel. He points out that "Moses sang, and led the people in singing. Miriam sang. Deborah and Barak sang, David sang, and wrote the Psalms to be sung. Jesus and the Twelve sang. Paul and Silas sang. The angels sing. In heaven EVERYBODY will sing." It could be said that "music is the language of every soul."

Godly music has even been used to literally change the course of the world. Halley says the public singing of Luther's hymns bore his preaching over central Europe and shook the world into the Reformation. Opponents of the Reformation wrote, "Luther has done more harm by his songs than his sermons," writes Seidel. It was also singing which made the Welsh revival great. "The Wesleyan revival was said to have been 'borne on the wings of song,'" according to Seidel. Was there ever a revival without it? The very best way now to rejuvenate dead churches would be to SING them into life.

Since God has given us such a wonderful gift in music, He expects His children to discern the good from the bad, the right from the wrong. As with everything in God's creation, Satan has corrupted music to suit his own purposes. Ungodly music, as godly music, has changed the course of the world. Allen Bloom writes, "Nothing is more singular about this generation than its addiction to music."

Music is one of the public spheres which Christianity deserted during the secularization process of the past 200 years. And we are paying the price, just as Israel did at the foot of Mount Sinai.

After God had given Moses the tablets of the Law, Moses and Joshua headed down the mountain.

"There is a noise of war in the camp," Joshua said (Ex 32:17). "It is not the noise of the shout of victory," Moses replied. "Nor the noise of the cry of defeat, but the sound of singing I hear" (Ex 32:18).

That idolatrous scene with the golden calf with its singing, dancing, and immorality made Moses so angry that he destroyed the tablets! It was their music which had alerted the two men to signs of corruption in the camp.

Our nation's music ought to also alert us to the awful corruption in our own land. Professor Bloom warns us that rock is "the youth culture and ... there is now no other countervailing nourishment for the spirit." Rock music "acknowledges the first emanations of children's emerging sensuality and addresses them seriously, eliciting them and legitimating them, not as little sprouts that must be carefully tended in order to grow into gorgeous flowers, but as the real thing. Rock gives children, on a silver platter, with all the public authority of the entertainment industry, everything their parents always used to tell them they had to wait for until they grew up and would understand later. . . . Never was there an art form directed so exclusively to children." As a result, today's youth have a worldview which is balanced on the sexual fulcrum! Satan is after the hearts of our children because he knows that what they think upon, they will become.

Offering the counterfeit of rock music with spiritual words to lure youth away from the hard stuff is not the answer. For "even when articulate speech is added, it is utterly subordinate to and determined by the music and the passions it ex-presses." With or without words, rock conveys a message which appeals to base emotions. "To attempt to portray biblical truths in such a vehicle is as contrary as hitching an ox with a don-key to plow a field. The team is unmatched in some very basic ways which can only lead to confusion. God is not the author of confusion," says Seidel.

Rather than tolerating Satan's counterfeits, we should teach children to value music which is true, noble, just, pure, lovely, and of good report. Music falls into two categories: music without words, and music with words. Each needs to be biblically evaluated to discern the good from the bad, the right from the wrong. The evaluation process evokes a lot of personal feelings. Sometimes, we can't even explain why we like or dis-like a particular musical work. Tastes differ greatly. Two people could be listening to the same piece, one thinking it a master-piece while the other winces in pain. Perhaps that is why God has given us so much variety.

We should therefore guard against defining music we like as "acceptable music," and music we dislike as "unacceptable." Instead, we should ask ourselves: "Can this music promote high and noble thoughts, peace, and praising God?" This applies not only to music which is offered directly to God but also to other forms which are pleasing as well as permissible.

Music should match the lyrics. Since music can stimulate good or bad emotions, the music and the lyrics both need to communicate the same message. For example, *Messiah*, by Han-del, is considered to have a perfect match of music and words. Both touch the entire spectrum of music, from serious to sad to exuberant. The greatest hymns do not focus upon entertainment or performance. They emphasize the magnification of the Lord and correct doctrine which lays the foundation for salvation and growth. An example of music's not matching the words would be teaming up a lighthearted, joyful melody with Psalm 51, which was written with a deeply contrite heart. The same would apply to Psalm 137 or Lamentations. Each involves a sorrowful setting which should be reflected in the music.

Musical lyrics also affect our speech "for out of the abundance of the heart the mouth speaks" (Matt 12:34). "Be filled with the Spirit, speaking to one another in psalms, hymns, and spiritual songs, singing in your heart **to the Lord**" (Eph 5:18-19).

"Let the word of Christ dwell in you richly in all wisdom, teaching and admonishing one another in psalms and hymns and spiritual songs, singing with grace in your hearts to the Lord" (Col 3:16).

In both passages, the words from psalms, hymns, and spiritual songs are to be spoken to one another as a means of edification. This is an outcome of first having them in our hearts, having repeatedly sung them to the Lord. They've been memorized. One outcome is that our speech will become seasoned with grace, which causes pleasure or delight, and this impacts how we speak to one another.

Note also that, in both instances, singing in psalms (Scripture set to music) is listed first. Satan scored a real victory when he erased the Psalms from Christian hymn books. With them went a lot of the biblical vocabulary, the richness of words written mostly by a man after God's own heart (1 Sam 13:14). Psalms has the widest variety of religious experiences in the entire Bible. And, being part of God's inspired Word, Psalms has an unreproachable theology, which can't be said of hymns or spiritual songs.

As a man after God's own heart, David showed us what it means to have a proper heart attitude before our holy and sovereign God. When His people stray, our music reflects our spiritual condition, and God says: "Take away from Me the noise of your songs, For I will not hear the melody of your stringed instruments" (Amos 5:23).

Music which focuses on feelings and personal experiences can be more man-centered than God-centered. This type usually lacks both theological and musical substance. God-centered music, in contrast, normally has strong theology as well as music theory.

Lyrics should be theologically correct. Theology, according to Webster, is the study of God and of religious doctrines and matters of divinity. In other words, the content of songs needs to be consistent with biblical truths. Sometimes songs we've sung for a lifetime may be strong on sentiment but weak on doctrine.

Consider the old Christmas favorite "We Three Kings of Orient Are." Nowhere in Scripture are we told the actual number of kings; nor did they visit the Christ child at the time of His birth. We should never take music for granted just because it is familiar.

From our children's earliest years, we ought to expose them to good music so they are trained to identify the genuine from the counterfeit. Does this mean they should never hear anything but that which is considered "sacred"? No. Developing a biblical world view is not divided into sacred-secular thinking patterns. As long as the music we listen to and expose our children to fits within the criteria stated above, we can be at peace. Martin Luther beautifully expresses:

> I wish to see all arts, principally music, in the service of Him who gave and created them. Music is a fair and glorious gift of God. I would not for the world forego my humble share of music. . . . I am strongly persuaded that after theology there is no art than can be placed on a level with music; for besides theology, music is the only art capable of affording peace and joy of the heart . . . the devil flees before the sound of music almost as much as before the Word of God.

Imagine the triumphant sound of victory when the greatest anthem of all times is sung in heaven as God's new song to His Lamb, slain before the foundation of the world!

> *"You are worthy to take the scroll, And to open its seals; For You were slain, And have redeemed us to God by Your blood Out of every tribe and tongue and people and nation, And have made us kings and priests to our God; And we shall reign on the earth" (Rev 5:9-10).*

> *"Worthy is the Lamb who was slain To receive power and riches and wisdom, And strength and honor and glory and blessing!" (Rev 5:12).*

> *"Blessing and honor and glory and power Be to Him who sits on the throne, And to the Lamb, forever and ever!" (Rev 5:13b).*

We can delight in God as His nature is revealed in every subject. And music is God's ultimate means for us to express our fullest delight in Him. Our praise and worship in the here and now is but a mere shadow of the immeasurable joy to come when we sing God's new song to our King of kings and Lord of lords! And we, beloved, have the precious privilege of planting in our own children the seeds of that joy in the Lord.

It begins with our own spiritual, moral, and academic development as parents. As disciples ourselves, we can best fulfill God's command to diligently teach all that He has commanded to our children — every waking moment of the day.

Part II: Making Disciples

Chapter Six

Nurturing in God's Word and His Ways

"Children, obey your parents in the Lord, for this is right. 'Honor your father and mother,' which is the first commandment with promise: 'that it may be well with you and you may live long on the earth.' And you, fathers, do not provoke your children to wrath, but bring them up in the training [nurture] and admonition of the Lord" (Eph 6:1-4).

NURTURING YOUR CHILDREN IN GOD'S WORD

Building disciples means teaching children to imitate Christ through the power of the Holy Spirit. Jesus always did those things which pleased His Father (John 8:29). Since Scripture reveals God's likes and dislikes, the only way to learn what pleases Him is to study the whole book. Departing from His Word is not pleasing to Him (Rom 8:8). Therefore, Christ's lambs need both head and heart knowledge of the Scriptures (Josh 1:8).

As with us, children are nurtured by teaching them to: hear, memorize, meditate, read, and study.

HEARING GOD'S WORD

In order to properly handle moral and academic training, our children need to begin with spiritual development. That development can begin, however, only when God quickens a child's spirit through salvation. The Scriptures are the means (Rom 10:17). Therefore, from the womb, we can begin nurturing our children in God's Word (2 Tim 3:15; Eph 6:4).

Manoah, for example, asked God to show Him what training He expected for Samson, who was still in the womb: "O my Lord, please let the Man of God whom You sent come to us again and teach us what we shall do for the child who will be born ...What will be the boy's rule of life, and his work (Judges 13:8, 12b)?" Manoah recognized that God must be the Teacher, the One to impart the judgment and knowledge needed to inculcate (impress and enforce) God's Word to train Samson "in the way he should go" (Prov 22:6).

God told Samson's mother to avoid wine and strong drink as long as the child was to have his nourishment from her, either in the womb or at the breast. Matthew Henry said this has both spiritual and physical significance.

Physically, abstention from alcohol during pregnancy and nursing protects the health and constitution of the baby. Henry showed a biblical recognition that infants are affected prior to birth. Modern medical research agrees. Pastor Stormer writes:

> *Actually you can even start getting your child ready for school and life even before he or she is born. Both the Bible and the "experts" indicate that your attitudes and actions even during the months before the birth have a real impact on a child's life. We probably have no idea how much a baby in the womb may know and feel and store up in his developing little mind.*

Stormer said experts have "determined that babies hear and react at least three months before birth. . . . These experts are just 'discovering' what the Bible said 2,000 years ago! The Bible records that three months before John the Baptist was born, he recognized the presence of the Lord Jesus Christ in the womb of the Virgin Mary." (See Luke 1:39-44.) He was also filled with the Spirit from the womb (Luke 1:15).

Once a child understands right from wrong and that disobediences are punished, he is old enough to understand salvation. He can associate sin's meriting a penalty with Christ taking that penalty in his stead on the cross. But we must be careful when talking with a little one about salvation. Some children pray the prayer of salvation for wrong reasons, just to please an adult or because they've seen someone else do it.

It has been my privilege to lead all four of my children to the Lord at tender ages. At the time of salvation, I told each, "If you really mean this prayer, then the Lord will save you. However, if you don't, then nothing happens." This prevents a false assurance of salvation simply because they mouthed the words. If it is genuine, you'll gradually see a change in life and attitudes.

Giving an invitation to a group of preschoolers in Sunday school or Christian school can result in "following the crowd" responses and risks making a child think he or she is being saved, when that is not the case. At RBCS I told the children that if anyone wanted to talk to me about the Lord to come at recess or snack time. If a child gave up something pleasurable to talk about salvation, the prayer usually proved genuine.

Sometimes conversion for young children in Christian homes is a gradual process. Conversion is not as dramatic for children as it is for adults. Thus, it is common to not even mention a salvation experience to either parent. Bringing a child to faith is God's responsibility. Our responsibility is to faithfully present the Word and trust the Lord for fruit in His own timing.

Family devotions are a main source for hearing the Word. Reading through the Bible sequentially also prepares for later understanding of the chronological order of history. Discussing the sequence of events aids development of reading comprehension skills. On portions commonly known as Bible stories, we should avoid using the term "Bible story," because some children associate "stories" with "pretend." Instead, refer to the Scripture reading as "the Bible account of. . . ." Occasional use of flannelgraph pictures can enhance the interest of extra young children.

Explanations are helpful for toddlers, as long as we don't talk down to them. Children "grow into" biblical vocabulary. Although the number of words acquired between age one (about four words) and two (300 words) is limited, "the ability to comprehend and understand speech is much greater than the number of words the child can say. This is particularly evident in bilingual families, where the vocabulary may be delayed, but comprehension in either language is appropriate."

As your children "grow into" the language of the Bible, watch for opportunities to correct any misunderstandings they might have acquired.

At times, these can be rather humorous. For example, a former RBCS kindergartner once came up to his teacher, in a dither, exclaiming: "Teacher! Travis is paying back evil for evil!" She gently queried, "Johnny, what's wrong?" Then came the real eye-opener: "Well, I kicked Travis — and he kicked me back!" Through Mrs. Kiser, Romans 12:17 came to life at that moment, for both boys.

Listening to some passages will naturally be more interesting than others. However, since every word has value, children should be trained to receive the whole counsel of God with respect. Ask the Holy Spirit to cause His Word to come to life as it is read. Enthusiasm for God's Word can influence the way our children accept and enjoy Bible readings.

Likewise, our delight in hearing the Word in our local assembly affects our children's. From birth, being in the house of the Lord regularly should be as natural as eating, playing, and sleeping. They need to be part of corporate worship, praise, and solid Bible preaching as early as possible. A good guideline as to "when" is the ability of a toddler to sit quietly and not be a distraction to others. In our family, we began by including a child during worship and praise, then gradually extending the time to a full service. Though a little one won't understand all that is going on, God's Word will not return to Him void (Isa 55:11). Even observing others during worship can help our children better comprehend what it means to reverence the Lord.

Learning to praise God through corporate and individual singing (especially with Scripture songs) is another vital part of children's growth: "Whoever offers praise glorifies Me . . ." (Psa 50:23). As early as possible, we should teach our children the most commonly sung music in our churches, because they will benefit more by participating in services with us. Singing His praises should be a part of every day. Music has tremendous teaching power. And an excellent way to end a busy day is to play a tape of soft Scripture songs at bedtime. This is especially good to quiet hearts after a bad dream.

MEMORIZING GOD'S WORD

Because hating evil is part of fearing God (Prov 8:13), memorizing Scripture is essential to avoid sinning (Psa 119:11). Work on memorizing individual verses by phrases. This prepares children for reading, which should be practiced in groups of words. Review regularly. Enrolling in a program like Bible Memory Association's is also valuable.

As our children mature, we can help them to form the discipline of memorizing longer passages of Scripture. Some beginning suggestions: Matthew 6:9-13 (the Lord's Prayer); Psalm 23; Exodus 20:1-17 (the ten commandments); 1 Corinthians 13 (love chapter); Romans 13 (understanding authority);

Hebrews 11:1-6, 12:1-7, 13:1-8 (purposes of chastening); Matthew 5-7 (sermon on the mount); plus anything in Proverbs. Working on these passages together as a family can be very rewarding for all concerned.

MEDITATING UPON GOD'S WORD

Helping our children establish a personal quiet time can prepare them for more mature meditation. As toddlers, you might begin by having them listen to a daily Bible reading from Alexander Scourby's tapes on *"The Holy Bible"* as they go down for a nap. Another suggestion is to record your own voice reading Scripture and perhaps singing a few Scripture songs. As your toddler matures, ask him or her to think carefully about the content of the reading and songs because you're going to ask some questions. This teaches the biblical principle of accountability (Rom 14:12).

Whichever method is chosen, be sure to convey that this is a very special time meant to bring great joy!

Because little children often meditate upon spiritual things, they need guidance toward right thinking. I recall a time that my son Randy was very deep in thought when he asked, "Mommy, will we look like this when we get to heaven?"

"Yes, Randy," I said. "The Bible teaches that when we get to heaven we'll know just as we are known (1 Cor 13:12)."

"But Mommy," he said quickly, "wouldn't you like to be pretty?"

His two-years-older brother came quickly to my defense by saying, " Well, Randy, Mom will be pretty when she gets to heaven because then her face will clear up!"

We can all laugh at such incidents, and you'll have plenty like them in your own family! The point is that meditation helps us spot faulty thinking in our children so that we can correct them biblically.

Prayer is another vital part of meditation. Teaching our children to praise God through prayer should be a top priority (Heb 13:15), because children need to develop thankful spirits (1 Thess 5:18). Even a little child can be taught to understand that God is in all our circumstances, working good for those who love Him (Rom 8:28). Understanding that truth should produce better responses to their everyday problems. It is important to teach by word and example that God is more concerned with how we respond to problems rather than with the problems themselves.

When Randy was just three, limited funds required that our family eat canned sweet potatoes every night for two weeks in a row. About the twelfth day, it was Randy's turn to ask the blessing. "Dear Lord," he said, "I pray that there aren't any sweet potatoes in heaven!"

His response was honest, but he needed a little guidance to help him be more thankful that we had anything to eat.

Teaching children how to meditate upon past as well as present blessings helps them to develop a proper attitude. "Bless the LORD, O my soul, and forget not all his benefits. . . ." (Psa 103:2). One way to remember God's benefits is to keep a "Blessings Book" in which each child records key prayer requests and answers (the "Yes's" as well as the "No's" and "Waits"). This not only builds faith in our children but also affects our children's children (Psa 78:1-7).

Such a Christian heritage for our grandchildren begins by presenting each of our children with his or her "Blessings Book" on the day of marriage. This album could also contain special pictures from birth to the wedding day. Encourage continuance of this tradition for the next generation.

Learning to talk to the Lord in the language of Scripture is a wonderful way to prepare for more mature meditation. Before a child can read, teach him to recall memorized verses and adapt those particular words to talking with God in a personal way. After reading skills are developed, show him how to use scriptural language in prayer by using an open Bible for reference and then adapting the wording as appropriate. We should pray for our children in their presence as well as with them. This can help them to acquire a better understanding of God's honoring prayers.

Keeping "clean accounts" with God as well as with others is an aspect of meditation, because it reflects upon individual responsibility before Him. Through example, we should first keep "clean accounts" with our children (1 John 1:9). Getting angry, not keeping our word, being inconsistent in correction and speaking harshly are all sins in God's sight. Confessing our transgressions is a prerequisite to God's hearing our prayers, as well as those of our children (Psa 66:18). By setting the example, we are more able to gently lead our children to also ask forgiveness of God, and those they have wronged (including us, when they disobey).

We should encourage faithful praying for all who have authority over our children that they may lead peaceful lives (1 Tim 2:1-2). If there is discord in our home, perhaps praying for authorities will help. Brothers and sisters should also be taught to pray for one another and for friends. As they learn to pray for one another they learn to love as Christ loves us. Prayers of importunity for the salvation of others is another example. The point is to develop an attitude of prayer without ceasing (1 Thess 5:17). Learning to meditate upon God's Word in this manner will heighten their understanding of biblical standards of living (Psa 119:99). In Joshua 1:8, we learn that meditation upon Scripture is the key to "success" (which also translates from the Hebrew into our English word "intelligence"). Remember: what a child thinks upon he will become.

Never Too Early

READING THE WORD

We should begin to build the desire in our children to read God's Word independently from infancy. This will help develop a positive attitude toward learning to read.

Thomas Nelson's *Precious Moments Bible* (New King James Version) is especially suitable for young children. The King James language has been retained except for replacing the *thee's, thou's, ye's, thy's,* and *thine's* (and similar archaic pronouns) with today's *you* and *your.*

Longer sentences have been shortened without taking anything away from the content, and 186 devotionals provided by Child Evangelism Fellowship have been included to help explain key passages.

In addition to a daily Bible reading schedule, opportunities should be provided for children to read the Bible at family devotions. "Sword Drills" can serve as an additional incentive to really get to know God's Word. You can do this by calling out a Scripture reference and timing how fast your child can find it. Then have the child read the verse. To avoid ungodly competition between siblings, rejoice in individual progress rather than "who's first." A great way to help children learn how to locate Bible references is to teach the names of the Books of the Old and New Testament through singing. *Wee Sing Bible Songs* is a good resource for this.

STUDYING GOD'S WORD

In addition to helping our children to establish a regular habit of daily Bible reading we should also teach them how to study the Scriptures as soon as they are able.

This can be done very simply by introducing them to a good chain reference Bible like Thompson's or *The Open Bible.*

Begin by showing the child how to look up other verses related to one being read. For example, next to Ephesians 6:1:

"Children, obey your parents in the Lord, for this is right," in *The Open Bible* are two references in Proverbs. The first conveys this similar thought: "My son, keep your father's command, And do not forsake the law of your mother" (Prov 6:20). The second is: "Listen to your father who begot you, And do not despise your mother when she is old" (Prov 23:22). Looking up related verses is easy to learn and will enrich Bible readings.

Another technique is to demonstrate a topical study using a chain reference Bible. Try to make it as practical as possible. For example, suppose your child is having a problem with lying. Using *The Open Bible*, you might have him look up "Liars, lies, lying" in the "Biblical Cyclopedic Index" and read all the verses listed under that section. Have him report back to you with his findings. If he has developed writing skills, have him write a paragraph or two about what he's learned. Later on, introduce other study aids as each child is ready for them.

If we feed Christ's lambs the Bread of Life without teaching them how to practically apply it, we will train them to be "hearers only" and not "doers" (James 1:22). Therefore, we must move beyond impressing to enforcing (applying Christ's mind to every aspect of our children's day). This involves biblical child training, which is the process of causing each child to come under our control and respect our word so that there is receptivity to being discipled in biblical principles.

NURTURING YOUR CHILDREN IN GOD'S WAYS

To effectively disciple Christ's lambs, we must see the child's nature through the eyes of God. Because His thoughts and ways are not like ours (Isa 55:8-9), God's view runs contrary to most humanistic theories dealing with human development, particularly those which address the behavior of children. Secular child development experts are thus "limited in their conclusion because they begin with an improper view of man. That is why their theories on how to raise children ultimately do not work and have to be constantly refined," according to authors Gary and Anne Marie Ezzo.[30]

The "experts" see children as born with a neutral nature which is prone toward neither good nor evil. God says children inherit Adam's sinful nature. At the time of his creation in God's image (Gen 1:26), Adam was perfect in his humanity. But Adam failed God's obedience test (Gen 2:17). Eve was deceived by the serpent (2 Cor 11:3); Adam was not (1 Tim 2:14). Adam willfully disobeyed God, and sin entered the world. Now man reproduces "after his kind." Therefore, each child, too, is born with a sin nature (Psa 51:5, Psa 58:3).

In *What the Bible Says . . . About Child Training* (a "must read" for every Christian parent), J. Richard Fugate says that "the nature of sin will motivate a child to do whatever bad, **or even good**, that he thinks will cause benefit to himself. When parents recognize that the natural, normal tendency of their child is to satisfy his own sinful nature, they are ready to become successful parents." (Emphasis added.)[31]

Under sin's control, the nature of a child is totally self-centered. He wants what he wants when he wants it. That spirit works totally against biblical discipleship, because Self is on the throne, and Self usurps Christ's rightful place (Deut 6:4, Matt 22:37-38). Self-pleasure crowds out love and consideration of others (Matt 22:39). Self-centeredness wars against Christ's command to deny self and forsake all for Christ (Luke 14:27, 33). In other words, self-centeredness does not submit to the Word of God (John 8:31-32).

The self-life can produce only corrupt fruit (Matt 7:17, 20). It is therefore imperative to teach each child that he is not "the center of his experience, . . . or his home," according to author Jack Fennema.[32] Rather, say the Ezzos, God's plan is that ". . . the woman alone completes the man, and man alone completes the woman. Children do not make a family unit —

they expand the family, they do not complete the family." Each child should therefore be taught that "he does not function for his own purposes. He must recognize that there is a God. There is an outside Force to whom he must respond. . . . Children are not to look inward for the ultimate answers to life. They are not to look outward on the horizontal plane either. They are to look upward to God in a dependent and creaturely way," explains Fennema.

Because of their sin nature, children don't naturally desire to be nurtured in that manner. So God placed them under the authority of their parents (Eph 6:1-3). Robert McCurry points out:

> GOD gives the parents, not the government, responsibility to care for and to train and educate their children according to His will and way. Parental authority is not a "right" conveyed by the state. It is an assignment, a responsibility, set forth by God's Word. The parent is to exercise authority over the child in keeping God's law. (Emphasis added.)[33]

Because God has established parents' authority as one of His ruling authorities on earth, children must be trained to do as they are told to do. A parent's word, under God's authority, is law. The Word of God is our only authority for child training. We must therefore function as those who have the right to rule under God.

Parents — not children — have the authority and responsibility to make the decisions of what to eat, when to sleep, which friends are wholesome, permissible activities, and what type of schooling. Untrained sinful natures, if left to themselves, will follow the world's path of "If it feels good, do it!" If we habitually indulge our children's wishes, they are in control of our home. That is cruelty, beloved, because sooner or later they will face God's judgment (and so will we).

Eli's whole household was judged severely, "For I have told him [Eli] that I will judge his house forever for the iniquity which he knows, because his sons made themselves vile, and he did not restrain them" (1 Sam 3:13).

Until children reach the place of independently functioning as disciples of Christ, they must be restrained by their parents. Restraint is a method of dealing with external immaturities until internal controls of discipleship can take over. The principle: A child will grow up in conformity with his sinful nature (self on the throne) if he is not restrained by his parents.

There are no guarantees of successful child training just because a child may be from a Christian home. Eli was a believer. He knew what his sons were doing and taught what was right (1 Sam 2:23-24). But training is more than "telling." As a father, Eli failed to fully inculcate God's Word through biblical training. He impressed upon his sons the Word of God, but he never enforced God's standards in their lives. He never trained them to obey. God says that "to obey is better than sacrifice" but "rebellion is as the sin of witchcraft, And stubbornness is as iniquity and idolatry" (1 Sam 15:22-23).

Children are unlikely to obey the invisible One until they have been trained to obey the visible *ones*. Without obedience, there is no true discipleship. Unless our children conform to what has been taught, they have not been trained.

Understanding childhood development helps us understand how to train our children for Christ. These four stages were identified by Christian educator J. Richard Fugate. He points out that "each of these stages has characteristics. Understanding the nature of a child should help parents realize the importance of their role of authority."

1. **Infant Stage:** This period applies until the infant is able to get around on his own. It is characterized by total dependence, defenselessness, and need of constant care.

2. **Child Stage:** This second stage refers to a little child in contrast to a youth in his teens. At this time, the child's greatest need is to know the "what." During this period, when most behavior patterns are set for life, a child will attempt to establish his own will as ruler. That is why it is so important for us to tell our children what is right to do according to God's Word and then require it to be done.

3. **Youth Stage:** The third stage is the period between ages 13 and 20. Now, the need for children to know the "why" behind the rules they are required to obey becomes important. A properly trained child will begin in his youth to operate more and more through internal controls as he learns to be responsible and accountable for himself. During this phase we ought to begin seeing fruit of biblical discipleship — a teen deciding to follow Christ instead of self.

4. **Adult Stage:** After the age of 20, a properly trained youth will honor his parents and their biblical training. He will be a disciple of Christ, who holds the biblical world view and possesses the godly character and academic skills necessary to fulfill God's calling and live to His glory.

Child training is serious business, because **a child learns obedience to parents as a preparation to obeying God.** The way our children respond to our God-given authority is the way they will respond to God and all authorities under God. We set either a positive or negative example of discipleship. We cannot be neutral. But we can train our children negatively by default (what we allow).

Poor table manners — sloppy eating, sloppy sitting, and sloppy speech are all examples of a basic attitude problem. God says: ". . . Whether you eat or drink, or whatever you do, do all to the glory of God" (1 Cor 10:31).

The problem is a lack of consideration for others, which ultimately is failing to love as He has loved us. Even a toddler can be trained to right habits. Ed and I had the pleasure of babysitting our oldest granddaughter, Amanda Leigh Claggett, for a weekend when she was only two. After church, we went to McDonald's for a snack. When we first sat down, though she LOVES french fries, she did not touch even one of them. Instead, she held out her hands and sweetly said, "Pray!" What a delight to see our children's godly training bearing fruit in *their* children! (By the way, Joe and Denise, who now have three beautiful daughters, began reading Scripture to their children in the womb.) The point is that the whole family should practice the presence of "the King of kings" at the dinner table as elsewhere.

Gossip is a major failure to love as He has loved us. Webster defines gossip as "tattling and telling news." Telling tales robs another of his good name, which God says "is better than precious ointment . . ." (Eccl 7:1).

Spurgeon says "the wounds of the tongue cut deeper than the flesh, and are not soon cured. Slander leaves a slur, even if it be wholly disproved." God tells us to "speak evil of no man" (Titus 3:2). From the time children first learn to speak, we must be alert to curb this sin. We must not play their "tattling" games. We must let them know right from the start that telling bad things about others is not God's way.

Set a positive example by speaking positively about them to others, protecting their reputation. Make comments about each of your children which can motivate them to do what is right because it is right. Focus upon the act (responsibility, generosity, orderliness, joyfulness) rather than the child to prevent building ungodly pride. When your child is within earshot, you could say to your husband, "I'm very pleased with how little Johnny is showing responsibility. He's been taking out the trash without being told, keeping his room clean, and watching out for his little sister. I'm sure the Lord is well pleased too."

Hypocrisy (pretending to be something we're not) is sin. God says each one of us is to "speak truth with his neighbor, for we are members of one another" (Eph 4:25).

Because the nature of children is to do whatever (bad or good) they think will benefit themselves, we should ask Jesus to help us discern hypocrisy. Again, we set the example (John 8:31–32).

Failing to enforce standards is most often manifested by overlooking wrongdoing. If we simply "do nothing" when a child violates God's standards, we mislead him to believe that whatever he wants to do is alright.

Sometimes we overlook our children's sins out of sheer laziness. Child training is WORK, but God says: "He who is slothful in his work is a brother to him who is a great destroyer" (Prov 18:9).

Or perhaps it is just inconvenient for us to correct the child at that moment. Children rarely misbehave at a convenient time. Try visiting with an adult in person or on the phone and watch what happens! Nevertheless, God's command is: "Children, obey your parents in all things, for this is well pleasing to the Lord" (Col 3:20). There is no loophole regarding timing.

Maybe we are just too tired. ". . . Let us not grow weary while doing good," God says, "for in due season we shall reap if we do not lose heart" (Gal 6:9). The choice is ours. We can deal with it now, when it's small, or later, when our children and their bad habits have grown, for "whatever a man sows, that he will also reap" (Gal 6:7).

A father who neglects his headship responsibility and puts the entire burden for child training on his wife is sinning against God and his wife.

"And you fathers, do not provoke your children to wrath, but bring them up in the training [nurture] and admonition of the Lord" (Eph 6:4).

Or perhaps mom spares the rod and waits until father comes home. This is also sin. "The rod and rebuke give wisdom, But a child left to himself brings shame to his mother" (Prov 29:15).

Beloved, God says: "Correct your son, and he will give you rest; Yes, he will give delight to your soul" (Prov 29:17). Biblical child training should be a team effort. Children quickly learn that God has commanded both parents to nurture them in His Word and His ways. (If your spouse is not a Christian, or if you are a single parent, biblical child training becomes more difficult. But with God's help it is not impossible. Consider the example set by Timothy's mother and grandmother.)

We can also intentionally train our children negatively. We can, for example, repeat commands two or three times. This tells our children they can ignore their parents the first couple of times. God considers this to be so serious that He warns "the eye that mocks his father, and scorns obedience to his mother, the ravens of the valley will pick it out, and the young eagles will eat it" (Prov 30:17).

DELAYED OBEDIENCE IS DISOBEDIENCE. To give the same instruction several times trains our children to not respond until we reach a certain frustration level. For example, an adult, carefully observing a little boy at play, watched to see what he'd do when his mother called him to come inside. The boy simply looked up and kept right on playing. She called again. Still no response. This continued for 10-15 minutes until finally the child obeyed. As the boy slowly sauntered up the sidewalk, the adult asked, "Son, why didn't you obey until just now?" The answer was standard: "Because Mom didn't really mean it until now!"

Remember, our children will learn to respond to God the way they are taught to respond to God's authorities on earth.

Threatening children to obey "or else" is also unbiblical. Scripture says that "masters," including parents as authorities, are to avoid "threatening" (Eph 6:9). Instead, masters and servants alike are to be "doing the will of God from the heart, with good will doing service, as to the Lord, and not to men" (Eph 6:6-7).

While threatening is bad, threatening without following through is even worse. This teaches that our word has no value. And, if we fail to keep our word, our children may well come to believe that God's Word has no value either. His scriptural warnings of consequences for sin become empty threats in the eyes of an untrained child.

Permitting a child to ignore instructions is training him to disobey. If children don't learn how to consistently obey, they can end up with bad reputations. People won't enjoy being around them. "Even a child is known by his deeds," God says, "whether what he does is pure and right" (Prov 20:11).

As little children grow in their knowledge of Christ, they are quick to recognize when Mommy and Daddy are ignoring God's instructions themselves. And they learn that being an adult means "Do as I say — not as I do."

Permitting a child to argue and question your instructions is strongly discouraged in 2 Timothy 2:23: "... Avoid foolish and ignorant disputes, knowing that they generate strife."

Parental authority is undermined when we allow our children to challenge it or question it. It is also undermined when our children witness us questioning God's authority or the authority of those God has placed over us.

Sometimes, there may be a legitimate reason to question an instruction. In these rare instances our children should be taught how to make a godly appeal. For example, my child might say, "Mother (or Father), may I make an appeal?" If the situation calls for immediate obedience, regardless of any new information, I might say, "No, I need you to obey me now, but

I'll be happy to discuss it with you later." If, however, I am able to listen right away, I will hear the appeal and then make a final decision based upon all the facts. In either case, my authority is not being undermined, and I avoid exasperating my son or daughter (Eph 6:4).

When our children wait to obey us, they are actually saying: "I will do your will when it becomes my will."

God says: ". . . Whoever does the will of my Father in heaven is My brother and sister and mother" (Matt 12:50).

Jesus showed how to obey the Father's will. It is the Father's will that children obey their parents. Children need to learn how to "deny self" by following instructions right away, and with a cheerful attitude. We prepare them to do His will by training them to first do our will — right away, not when they "feel like it." We in turn set the example by obeying God's will right away (and not when we "feel like it").

Asking a child "Why?" he did or didn't do something trains him to reject responsibility for his own actions. God says: "He who is faithful in what is least is faithful also in much; and he who is unjust in what is least is unjust also in much" (Luke 16:10).

To teach responsibility, we should ask questions like: "What did you do?" "What does God's Word say should have been done?" and "How could you handle this differently the next time?"

Every one of us will one day give account to God (Rom 14:12). Are we faithful to our Lord in even the smallest tasks? How about the big ones — like discipling His heritage for Christ's sake? Or do we give "excuses" for not doing as He's commanded?

TRAINING A CHILD

"Control is the force, or pressure, by which you exercise your right of parental rulership — the right to set the standards for, to direct the actions of, and to administer justice to your children. As a parent, you have the responsibility and legitimate right to exert pressure on your children," says Fugate.

Control is divided into three functions. The first is the power to direct. This is the use of force necessary to cause the child to follow your directions. The second function is the power to *restrain*. This is the use of pressure to hold him back from what he would do if left to his own will. *Pressure* is the third function, which results from the restricting rules (standards) given to the child for which he is tested and judged.

Controlling a child is an expression of parental love, a true concern for the benefit of a child. This is the agape form of love, a commitment to act in the best interest of another. In exercising agape love, you do so for the benefit of the child, whether it "feels good" to him or not. Genuine love will pay the price. It means living with unplanned interruptions and inconveniences, curbing our own desires in order to train in every correction situation.

Training begins in infancy, with obedience to simple commands like "No," "Stop," and "Come." This training could even save a child's life. This was certainly true for Anne Welton, an RBCS elementary teacher. Anne once shared that when her daughter Lisa was very young, Lisa's instant obedience to the command "Come!" spared her from a possible shark attack at a Florida beach.

As we train our children, we will learn to discern between immaturity and rebellion.

For instance, finding out your child spread peanut butter on bread and then put it into the toaster (as our son Randy did) is not rebellion. Nor is cleaning the bathroom toilet with the kitchen sponge and then washing the dishes with it (as did Randy). Nor is having a contest with a younger sister to see who can let the dog lick their teeth the longest. (Guess who won?) Keeping a sense of humor can make those times a lot more bearable.

Another example is the accidental destruction of property. When one of our children carelessly clowns around and damages or destroys something in the process, this is not rebellion. However, it should be dealt with. And this requires the biblical principle of restitution.

Restitution is rooted in the eighth commandment: "You shall not steal" (Ex 20:15, Deut 5:19). The earth and all it contains belongs to God (Psa 24:1), who created man in His image and instructed him to exercise dominion over it (Gen 1:26, 28). *Stewardship* is to be exercised in accordance with God's principle of justice which recognizes God as the One giving man power to make wealth (Deut 8:7, 18). As such, He has laid down rules for restitution (Ex 21:34-22:17; Lev 5:15-16, 6:2-5, 24:17-23; Num 5:5-8; Deut 22:1-4).

What all that basically means is this. Whether the damage was accidental or intentional, our children should make it right. This applies to losing things as well. This can mean cleaning up a mess, "helping" to repair the item or working to earn money to personally pay for its replacement.

Rebellion, on the other hand, is the willful rejection of authority — either actively or passively. It is a conflict of two opposing wills. Passive rebellion is more difficult to spot and to deal with. ("Sweet" little girls are especially good at this.)

Chastisement is the force defined in God's Word to be used by parents to control children when they rebel. Chastisement is specifically limited to the infliction of pain for correction or restraint. Chastisement expresses parental love. "He who spares his rod hates his son, But he who loves him disciplines [chastises] him promptly" (Prov 13:24).

When a child is in rebellion, physical pain (chastisement) is usually the only pressure that will cause him to choose to accept parental direction and control. A selfish love wants an easier way. Selfish sentiment toward the child is to spare ourselves the pain of seeing a child endure suffering and disappointment. A self-giving love realizes obedience must come at cost and pain. God says: "Now no chastening seems to be joyful for the present, but painful: nevertheless, afterward it yields the peaceable fruit of righteousness to those who have been trained by it" (Heb 12:11).

The pain of the rod protects our children from the pain they could certainly suffer later when God is forced to chastise them. Chastisement must be applied biblically. Use a rod to inflict pain sufficient enough to cause a child to correct his rebellion or to restrain the child from willful disobedience. If a child repeatedly disobeys, perhaps the rod was not applied properly.

CAUTION: NEVER use chastisement as a means of venting your own anger because your child dared to defy you. Chastisement must always be for the benefit of the child. The objective of chastisement is always to bring the will of a rebellious child under control, not cause suffering. Here is a biblical guideline to follow:

1. When your child is guilty of rebellion (willful disobedience), first ask: "What did you do?" and "What does God's Word say should have been done?" Counsel with Scripture so that he understands why he is being chastised. Show the applicable verse in the Word. Have him read or follow along as you read. This method will make Scripture take on more meaning as you practically apply it to real life situations.

2. Guide your child to confess his sin to God (agree with God that it is sin) and ask forgiveness. When fear of the chastisement preoccupies his mind, you may need to pray for him. After he's settled down, then have him pray as well. (Steps One

and Two also give *you* a chance to "settle down" before applying the rod so you don't do so in anger but for the good of your child.)

3. Explain that "love" demands he be chastised for his good ("God is love" [1 John 4:8]). Have the child bend over and grab his ankles. Wrap your hand around to hold his hands in a position which will not permit them to get free. Apply the rod with enough strength for the child to feel it, and not want a repeat application. (This does not mean child abuse.) Use of a small flexible wooden dowel will sting but not do damage.

4. If proper heart submission and obedience follows the application of the rod, restore fellowship with him by comforting and cuddling him in your lap. Talk about ways to handle the same situation differently next time so that the correction becomes a positive learning experience.

Does the above procedure take into account the differences in children? For the most part, yes. "For whom the LORD loves He chastens, And scourges every son whom He receives. If you endure chastening, God deals with you as sons; for what son is there whom a father does not chasten?" (Heb 12:6-7).

Occasionally, a very strong-willed or extra sensitive child may not respond as well to spankings as to other methods, such as isolation in a bedroom, withdrawal of a privilege, being made to sit still in a chair for a specified period of time, etc. My daughter, now Shari Turner, has five-year-old twins, Michael and Lauren, who are both precious (of course!) but real opposites in temperament. Michael is very strong-willed; Lauren is extra sensitive. Lauren shapes up rather quickly to a spanking, but the application of the rod only seems to make matters worse with Michael. He responds much faster to having to sit still in a chair for five or ten minutes, or being sent to his room. So alternate methods are used for most offenses, but Shari and her husband, Mark, believe that spanking is still appropriate for more serious rebellion.

What about the strong-willed child who likes to throw temper tantrums when disappointed or opposed? If you avoid chastisement, you'll train this type to scream for what he wants. He will never be able to handle a variety of circumstances. How can temper tantrums be stopped?

A classic example is what happened when our son, Randy, was two-and-a-half. Randy had had to face quite a few adjustments the previous year. His daddy was in Vietnam, we moved three times, a new sister arrived at a time when Randy was seriously ill and I wasn't there for him. By the time Ed returned from the war, Randy didn't even remember him. Over the next few months, he started throwing frequent temper tantrums.

Nothing Ed and I tried had worked until God directed us to a wise physician who suggested we throw ice cold water in his face when he had a tantrum. As a mom, that sounded harsh, and I hated the thought of it. Nevertheless, the next time Randy threw himself down and started to scream, I calmly got a small glass of water which had been sitting on a shelf in the refrigerator. Walking over to where he was kicking, I simply dumped it in his face and then walked off without a word. Randy immediately jumped up, with hands on his little hips, and said, "Mommy, I'm mad at you! You got me all wet!"

I gently replied, "Well, son, I'm not exactly pleased with you either right now. Every time you throw yourself down and kick and scream I'm going to do the same thing again."

He tested my word about two weeks later but quit at once when he saw me walk toward the refrigerator door.

Now, we face a similar situation with one of our adorable granddaughters, Victoria (pictured on the cover of this book), who is both strong-willed and extra sensitive. Victoria's basic temperament is very complex, and her dear parents, Lynda and Tony (also on the cover) have to go to the throne of grace often to know how to guide her God's way. Like Randy, she has been through a lot recently — the arrival of baby brother, Gabriel, being very sick when he was born, having a two-year-old cousin visit for 10 days shortly thereafter, then her mommy having surgery, and now an upcoming move to another state. Her frustration often comes out in some really big fits, which though understood, still must be curbed. Nothing has worked but ice cold water. The first time the ice water was dumped in her face, she responded much like Randy did. She hated getting wet, stood up immediately, and said so. But so far, it looks like this method is once again going to prove a God-send.

During one of his child-training seminars, Richard Fugate also recommended ice cold water for dealing with temper tantrums. He explained that there is a physiological reason for a little one to respond to the ice water by stopping the tantrum. And he has received confirmation of this from parents all over the country. If you're having trouble along this line, I recommend praying about it and then giving it a try. However, be patient. Results will vary from child to child. It may take several times before tantrums cease altogether.

Now, what about the sensitive or emotional child who cries at the drop of a hat? Normal tendency is to excuse poor behavior because of the child's sensitivity. But the sensitive child will also often escape into tears when he doesn't want to obey. "No chastisement" for this type child will train him to give in to his emotions.

My husband and I know how difficult it is to chastise the sensitive child. You see, not only was Randy strong-willed, but his artistic temperament also made him extra sensitive. During the time Randy began throwing the tantrums he also developed bouts of colitis. Remembering all he'd been through the previous year tempted us to give "excuses" for his poor behavior. But, praise God, even though we were still young Christians at the time, He provided insight to understand that if we ignored Randy's disobediences as a little one, he would be more difficult to correct later on.

Was it hard? Very hard. Because of his mischievous nature, Randy ended up getting in trouble more than our other three children combined. (Life would have been very dull without him!) In his immaturity, he sometimes felt we didn't love him because he didn't see his brother and sisters being corrected as frequently. He was just too young to realize that it was love which motivated us to pay the temporary price of his not understanding in order to train Him in God's ways. Was it worth it all? Yes! Now in his late twenties, Randy has thanked us often for hanging in there with him. As the father of a very sweet, very active two-year-old daughter, Shannon (who is also prone to temper tantrums), he more fully understands the love behind the price we paid. Ed and I are so very proud of Randy, who has become a great husband and father! And we both enjoy very fond and happy memories of Randy's childhood, as we do with all our children.

Another example of the sensitive child is one who loses control and gets in an emotional state when he or she doesn't want to do something. What can you do? Try giving a "count to 3" before dealing with him more firmly. This recognizes his immaturity without overlooking the requirement for obedience. However, if no immediate response is gained, apply the rod in love.

The "count-to-3" technique can also work wonders with other types of misbehavior. With our own four, rarely did the count go past "one" because they knew we meant business. This technique is especially good when a child starts to whine. Whining works against God's command to "Do all things without complaining and disputing" (Phil 2:14). When our children tried whining, we told them that if they didn't stop by "three," we'd give them a reason to cry. (Whining is immaturity; refusing to stop whining would then become rebellion.) This was so effective that whining never became a problem with any of them.

A word of caution from personal experience: one day Ed told our firstborn, "You've got until the count of three to stop." I started giggling, and Ed glanced at me with a puzzled look. I laughingly replied, "Joey doesn't even know how to count yet!" The point is to make sure that your children are capable of following through with whatever you ask of them. Once you know they can, then be consistent in holding them to it.

All types of children require consistent biblical training because they are responsible to God for their own behavior and attitude. Therefore, over and over teach this truth: "Regardless of the circumstances, God holds you responsible for your own attitude." This does pay off. Shari once told me, "Mom, every time I think about fussing with Mark, I hear you saying, 'Regardless of the circumstances, God holds you responsible for your attitude.' And then I get my attitude right." Following that guideline alone can solve a lot of relationship problems! (By the way, in his application for seminary in 1994, Mark gave a tender testimony that Shari's godliness when they were courting had inspired him to get more serious with the Lord. Ed and I continually rejoice over how much both of them have grown in the Lord during their 9 years of marriage!)

There is a season for everything under heaven. There is a season for us to control our children, and, if we are faithful to do this according to God's instructions, there will be a season in which our children are able to control themselves.

A CHILD IS FOR MOLDING

I took a piece of plastic clay,
And idly fashioned it one day,
And as my fingers pressed it still,
It bent and yielded to my will.

I came again when days were past,
The bit of clay was hard at last.
The form I gave it still it bore,
But I could change that form no more.

I took a piece of living clay,
And gently formed it day by day,
And molded it with power and art
A young child's soft and yielded heart.

I came again when years were gone:
He was a man I looked upon.
The early imprint still he bore,
But I could change him then no more.

Anonymous

Chapter Seven

Getting Off to a Right Start: Birth to Three

"For no other foundation can anyone lay than that which is laid, which is Jesus Christ" (1 Cor 3:11).

Children don't wait to learn. Therefore, we shouldn't wait to teach. Why, how, and what we teach them can be an act of worship when motivated by a desire to show God how much He is worth to us.

Jesus Christ, the King of kings and Lord of lords, is worth whatever it takes to train our children to fulfill His calling and live for His glory! To do so requires instilling in them the biblical world view and the godly character and the necessary academic skills.

". . . I will give [Samuel] to the LORD all the days of his life," said Hannah (1 Sam 1:11). Hannah's spirit as a mother was beautiful. From birth, we should likewise begin an instruction process which returns our children to God.

Hannah's training of Samuel during his first two to three years laid the foundation for lifetime service for God. More and more, it is evident that what happens in the home during the first thirty-six months can largely determine how well a child will do educationally, and in life as a whole. Developing disciplined and obedient minds in early childhood is the first step toward Christian maturity as well as academic excellence. Structure is a valuable building block in this whole educational process.

Biblically, from the moment they are born, children must learn to submit to God's laws. No one is ever free to do just as he pleases. This is consistent with the basic principle of discipleship: in order to save our lives, we must lose them (Matt 16:25).

If, right from the start, structure is a normal part of our children's lives, they accept it as "that's life." Thus, they never form the habit of "doing their own thing." Structure, in that sense, means actively, constantly, and purposefully training children to be receivers of what they ought to learn — not deciders of what *they* will learn and when.

Even newborns need some structure. For example, if we continually give in to an infant's demands (in contrast to genuine needs), we train by default that the world revolves around him. Facts are that the world does not. And that truth needs to be learned from the beginning.

Discipline and order are two of the greatest gifts we can give our children. We should therefore discipline them to curb their "I want what I want when I want it" natures.

As you get to know your newborn's needs vs. wants, establish a general routine for baby that fits the rest of the family's schedule. As much as possible, provide regular feeding times, nap times, bedtimes, and so forth. Some flexibility, as when sickness occurs, is certainly appropriate. However, as a rule, a loving, structured atmosphere with well-planned days is our wisest stewardship of time (Eph 5:15-16).

FOR THE BEST START

In addition to building their spirits and character, what ought we to be teaching between birth and three? Teaching the finest language skills possible will combine with their spiritual/moral development for the best start in life.

The main purpose of language is to facilitate knowing the Word and the ability to make Him known. We exist for His pleasure (Rev 4:12).

> *"Man shall not live by bread alone, but by every word that proceeds from the mouth of God,"* says the Word *(Matt 4:4).*
>
> *"Has God indeed said. . . ?"* refutes Satan *(Gen 3:1).*

Satan and His forces of darkness are at war with the Word (Eph 6:10-14)! Unable to destroy Christ at Calvary, the devil is now out to destroy His offspring. And the early childhood years are the front lines of the battle.

From birth, we should therefore begin laying a foundation which enables our children to recognize that God's world is a spiritual battleground, not a playground.

Through four basic areas we can begin reclaiming lost territory as a result of Satan's attacks on reading, writing, and mastering words. We should:

1. Whet our children's appetites to know both the written and living Word.
2. Develop our children's vocabulary to facilitate knowing Him and the ability to make Him known.
3. Equip our children with skills to read, comprehend and obey the Word, as early as God-given capabilities allow.
4. Equip our children with skills to write well, for the Word's sake.

By developing each child's spirit, character, and mind in terms of recognizing the sovereign authority of the Word over his or her life, we provide a foundation for becoming living sacrifices. When such biblical priorities are established, everything else falls into its proper perspective.

Like Timothy, from the womb onward, the Holy Spirit can begin whetting our children's appetites to know the Word. Reading (and talking) to baby before and after birth gets him or her used to the pleasure of listening.

Such a child is best prepared for listening to and thus following instructions, a prerequisite for learning to read, comprehend, and obey the Word. The importance of this cannot be overstated.

At Rocky Bayou Christian School (RBCS), it is easy to spot children whose parents have spent time reading to and talking with them, compared with those left to themselves a lot. Because the latter never learned to listen in the home, often they were developmentally delayed, or even learning disabled. Both behavior and communication skills have been poor in such children. By hampering language development during those tender years, Satan had already gained the upper hand.

DEVELOPING LANGUAGE SKILLS

How can we develop the finest language skills possible? First, keep in mind that a little child's ability to understand language is several years beyond his ability to give it back. Therefore, "baby talk" and talking down to a child should be avoided.

An important educational principle is this. We should consistently nurture children with correct information, whether they understand it at the moment or not. (Hebrew and Colonial parents followed this same principle.) Such teaching moments are like "coat hangers for the future." According to each child's timetable, these "hangers" will be sorted by the Lord into the right closets for it all to make sense.

Building listening skills is the forerunner of acquiring language. Since structure should be a normal way of life, we should make (and keep) a plan to provide daily listening activities.

A ticking clock by baby's crib for a little while each day can get his listening attention. So can shaking a rattle, squeezing a squeaky toy, playing a music box, or winding up a toy which makes sounds. Taking baby outside to listen to birds chirping, frogs croaking, crickets, and so forth, can also foster alertness.

Equally important is visual stimulation. Initially, this can be done by hanging brightly colored "eyecatchers" at cribside. A crib mobile is a good idea. One with Noah's ark, animals, lambs, or butterflies is colorful and also provides an opportunity to talk about the Lord's creation. The "eye catchers" and location should be changed every week or so. Noticing details in infancy will pay off later when learning to distinguish one letter or word from another.

When we talk with baby, perhaps while cuddling or carrying him around the house, we should name common objects around him: a Bible, parts of the body, clothes, bed, food, furniture, appliances, people, toys, and other interesting objects. Taking walks outdoors is great for naming specific things God created, such as animals, birds, fish, insects, cocoons, butterflies, leaves, and grass. Either of these techniques is good for distracting a baby who is fussing to eat or nap earlier than normal.

Naming things God created reminds me of a trip to the bank with our Lynda when she was two. This particular bank gave a lollipop to children after a parent's banking transaction. She knew that fact.

"God made the sky; God made the water; God made the trees; God made the beautiful flowers," I was pointing out along the way.

"God made lollipops!" she suddenly and excitedly called out. Lynda had concluded that since He created all the things I was mentioning, He must be responsible for the lollipop she anticipated.

Her theology was not that far off, since He is the giver of every good gift (James 1:17). Even a little child can be taught to have a thankful heart, recognizing God as the ultimate Source of both the big and little joys of life. (Just this morning, Lynda's own two-year-old, Victoria, was so thankful for a special breakfast cereal that she not only thanked God for it but also asked her mommy and daddy to pray to thank Him again!)

As the ability to speak develops, saying words after us as we point to objects, almost in drill fashion, works well. Over a period of time, we should do this repeatedly until the words become part of our children.

Preparing a cassette tape of common sounds such as a siren, door opening/closing, birds chirping, bee buzzing, phone ringing, tea kettle whistling, teeth being brushed, gargling, meat frying, or alarm clock ringing is also great. A game could be played to see how many sounds can be named. To maintain interest and increase listening ability, the content should be changed periodically. Later on, we can enjoy helping our toddler classify naming words into "alive" and "not alive."

Adding "describing words" to our children's vocabulary can also be fun. Young children like the challenge of learning that words can be classified by size, color, weight, appearance, and so forth. "Describing words" tell how something looks, smells, tastes, feels, and so on.

We should use this type of questioning: "What is the name of this?" "What color is it?" "What is its size?" "How does it smell?" And so forth.

Identifying and describing kitchen foods while preparing a meal is one example of an opportune time to develop this skill. This also keeps a toddler constructively occupied. As our children are ready, preparing meals together is an excellent time to develop responsibility plus develop math skills.

Of course, we will want to especially emphasize words which describe God, including character qualities which please or displease Him (for instance, being wise, honest, good, bad, obedient).

For variety, a good rainy day activity is to put a collection of small common objects into a paper sack, such as a cotton ball, empty spool of thread, piece of sandpaper, rubber worm from Daddy's fishing box, grape, pacifier, coaster, sponge, plastic flower, lemon, and rock. With eyes closed, a child should reach into the sack and try to identify each item by shape, feel, smell, or taste.

Action words are another favorite with little children. In fact, they love to act out "doing words" like jump, hop, skip, crawl, walk, and run. They also enjoy looking at "action" pictures and having us ask what is happening in the picture. When cause/effect reasoning enters in, this can be discussed simply (for example, a kitten knocked over a flower pot and dirt spilled on the rug).

Discussing things to do as a family (picnic, trip to Grandma and Grampa's house, cleaning the yard, activities in various types of weather) is another opportunity to discuss "doing words." So is naming specific things that God does. Or things He wants us to do (such as love, obey, pray, read).

Toddlers especially enjoy the challenge of listening for and making up their own rhyming words. Rhymes and little children just naturally go together. They never seem to tire of repetition. They love to recite over and over (and over and over) — and to act out rhymes.

Due to the nature of rhymes (and short poems), these are excellent resources for identifying nouns, verbs, and adjectives. It is best, however, to focus mostly on rhymes and poems which teach about the Lord. One good resource for this is Emily Hunter's *The Bible Time Nursery Rhyme Book* (Manna Publications, 1981).

During the course of our day, as opposites come up, we can point these out or demonstrate them as appropriate. For example, baby is "little"; sister or brother is "big." We can "open" the lid to the toy box to get a toy out; we "shut" the lid after we put the toy away. Dad may be walking "ahead"; children are walking "behind." We should work "first" and play "last." We should read the Bible from its "front" cover to its "back." God has no "beginning" or "end." Jesus makes our "rough" ways "smooth." We should walk a "straight" not "crooked" path for His sake. Jesus wishes we were either "hot" or "cold" in our love for Him, but not lukewarm. God wants "clean" not "dirty" hearts. Even children are known by whether they are "obedient" or "disobedient." We should love "good" and hate "evil." When we "lose" our life we will "find" it.

We can have fun helping our children learn to associate words, thus further enhancing their thinking skills. Some examples: cup/saucer, ice cream/cone, pot/lid, tea/tea kettle, shoes/socks, sun/moon, mother/father, sister/brother, horse/saddle, and so on. As they grow, these type relationships can be included: "Small is to little as big is to (large)"; "toes are to feet as fingers are to (hands)"; "man is to woman as boy is to (girl)"; "start is to stop as begin is to (end)"; "mother is to aunt as father is to (uncle)." Both can make wise use of time while traveling.

Identifying whether an object is singular (one) or plural (more than one) also lays an important foundation. We can use everyday examples like socks, shoes, belt, kittens, dog, baby, or cupcakes. As we look through magazines or books, we can point to pictures and have our toddler tell whether illustrated objects are singular or plural.

A very natural outcome of teaching singular and plural words is introducing number concepts. Even an activity like folding clothes together can be a neat teaching opportunity. As clothes are sorted and classified, one-of-a-kind items can be named "singular." More than one can be named "plural." Clothes can then be sorted, counted, stacked, described by color, size, shape, smell (such as, fresh, lemony, flowery, powdery). Putting sorted clothes away together combines a lesson in God's orderliness with being responsible.

"Johnny, please bring me one diaper for the baby." "Susie, please get three napkins for lunch." "Would you please stack these four books neatly on the shelf?" "Please get five knives, forks, and spoons and finish setting the table." "You may choose two favorite toys to play with right now; the rest should remain in the toy box until those are put back."

Instructions like these develop listening skills, obedience, as well as number concepts. When giving an instruction, we should first make sure we have our child's attention. He should repeat the instruction to prevent his saying "I didn't hear you." Carrying the instruction out right away avoids the claim, "I forgot."

As soon as a child can follow one direction well, we can add two at a time, then three. During the initial training process of adding extra instructions, this could be done as a game. After the ability to follow more than one direction is consistently demonstrated, we should lovingly hold a child accountable to follow through.

SHARE THE JOY OF READING

Reading (or telling) stories effectively builds listening skills and increases vocabulary. Highest on the list should be Bible stories. Reading the "Bible account of . . ." regularly can further whet our children's appetites for learning to independently read the Word. Since little ones love repetition, they never seem to tire of these. The "Condensed Cyclopedia of Topics and Texts" in Thompson's *The New Chain-Reference Bible* (see #1672) contains a handy list entitled "Bible Stories for Children."

It is helpful to discuss a Bible account's context (such as, the culture "long ago;" the characters such as father, mother, grandmother, brother, sister, uncle; describe places; explain objects not common to our day). Whenever possible, pictures from Bible study aids can be included. Questions about story sequence will enhance reading comprehension skills.

After the reading, we can teach letter sounds by identifying key words from the Bible account which start with a particular sound.

"Do you hear /s/ at the beginning of 'Samuel'?" we might say. (Emphasize the /s/ at the beginning of "Samuel.") If he does not, we should simply respond, "Yes, we hear /s/ at the beginning of 'Samuel.'" Patience is needed because this listening skill takes time to develop.

Children three and under commonly seem to know something one day and not know it the next. But this should not deter us from teaching. By age four it is likewise common for "coat hanger" teaching prior to that age to be hung in the proper closets. In other words, it all suddenly "clicks." And when that moment happens, it is very exciting!

In addition to Bible readings, they should also be exposed to the richness of a wide variety of wholesome reading materials.

The way we read is also crucial. Good reading sounds like talking. Therefore, we should use good expression, observe punctuation marks carefully, and enunciate clearly. Because children imitate adults, our example affects the quality of their future reading skills as well as enjoyment. It can make a difference between growing up to read only what they have to or because they truly want to. That, in turn, affects their relationship to the Word.

Vocabulary will increase tenfold by age four as long as our children are talked to, listened to, and read to regularly. During this process, as each learns to speak, we should gently correct poor pronunciation, sloppy grammar, and slang terms, being careful to set a proper example. However, this should be done in accordance with capabilities. The younger the child, the less we can expect.

Acquiring an extensive vocabulary does not mean that young children will understand word usage initially. For instance, when our Shari was little, she picked up a can of "Hard to Hold" hair spray. She read the label, then, with a puzzled look on her face, stated, "No it's not. . . ." Having an extensive vocabulary can make us think children are more mature than they really are. We should be careful not to expect more than we ought. They need time to "grow into" the vocabulary.

The areas discussed so far form a basis for academic excellence. Each has a "coat hanger" purpose which will fit into a particular academic closet later on. For instance, learning about "naming," "doing," and "describing" words fits into the closet of identifying the "who," "doing," and "what" of sentences. Using grammar as a tool to build reading comprehension is highly effective.

PREPARING FOR FORMAL
READING INSTRUCTION

Additional preparation for formal reading instruction can begin informally, somewhere around age one. Learning sound/symbol relationships is the first step. Since the short vowel sounds are the first sounds an infant makes, I recommend starting there.

At the same time each day (once or twice daily), about five minutes could be spent teaching sound/symbol relationships. A regular schedule establishes a routine which conveys that learning is an important part of "that's life."

First, begin working on only one sound. For example, hold up a block with the letter *Aa* on it, then smile while pointing to the letter and saying its short sound. (No letter names should be taught at this point.) Showing great approval once baby can respond with a similar sound encourages him to do so again. Giving him the block to hold after each session rewards attentiveness. When the child is ready, move on to the *Ee, Ii, Oo,* and *Uu* blocks.

Another technique is to use alphabet flashcards. Our daughter, Lynda, took the *Christ-Centered Alphabet Wall Cards* (Christ Centered Publications, 1986) and placed them back to back, laminated them, then punched three holes on the left for metal rings so that a small "letters" book was formed. During reading times with Victoria, Lynda also spends a few minutes on letter sounds, then talks about the spiritual pictures and rhymes on the cards. Victoria knows all the letter sounds and enjoys identifying the letters in other reading materials.

At RBCS, the short vowel sounds are reviewed by singing "Noah's Vowel Song." We use a visualized chart illustrating Noah's ark plus five animals whose names contain the short vowels (cat, hen, pig, dog, and duck).

"Just as God created animals which make sounds, like those pictured on this chart, so He created letters with sounds," the teacher explains.

She then reviews the story of Noah, to include the fact that the five animals pictured on the chart were among the animals God sent to the ark. Children then enjoy making the animal sounds, followed by the sounds of the vowels in the middle of their names.

The teacher points to the appropriate vowel in each animal's name as the children sing:

NOAH'S VOWEL SONG

Godly Noah built an ark;
/ă/, /ĕ/, /ĭ/, /ŏ/, /ŭ/.
Built it out of gopher bark;
/ă/, /ĕ/, /ĭ/, /ŏ/, /ŭ/.
And to that ark God sent a cat,
A meow, meow, meowing furry cat.
With an /ă/, /ă/ here and an /ă/, /ă/ there,
And an /ă/, /ă/ everywhere.

The remaining vowels are taught by substituting each vowel sound with its corresponding animal: a "cluck, cluck, clucking laying hen," an "oink, oink, oinking muddy pig," a "woof, woof, woofing friendly dog," and a "quack, quack, quacking fluffy duck." This method combines learning the short vowel sounds with biblical truth.

Sound/symbol practice can be accomplished by mixing the vowel letter blocks. First, call out a sound (auditory discrimination). Then help your child select the block containing the letter which represents that sound (visual discrimination). Once each is identified, assist his stacking the letter blocks one on top of another.

Teaching the consonant sounds should be added slowly. This order of introduction has proven effective: *Ss, Mm, Ff, Rr, Nn, Gg, Bb, Tt, Pp, Dd, Hh, Ll, Cc, Kk, Jj, Ww, Vv, Qq, Xx, Yy,* and *Zz*. Introduce each consonant as rapidly as your child's God-given capabilities allow.

For teaching variety, magnetic letters on a refrigerator door can be used (or a stove top protector covered with solid-colored contact paper). The letters can be positioned on the right. Have your child move the letter standing for the sound called out to the left side. (Flannelgraph letters on a thick piece of cardboard covered with flannel also work well.)

As the consonant sounds are learned, a beginning reading/spelling exercise can be accomplished easily by this method. For example, call out the sound of the letter *s*; have your child slide the *s* to the left. Call out the short sound of the letter *a*; have him slide the *a* to the left. Then give assistance reading the blend of the two letters. Have your child add an ending consonant, such as *t*, to make a word out of the blend. Conclude by helping him read the word ("sat" in this case) and use it in a sentence about God's Word or His ways — for example, "Jesus loved the little children who once sat on His lap." Stacking blocks as sounds are identified, sliding magnetic letters, or using a flannelboard nearby can also be done while preparing a meal. This keeps a child out from under foot plus uses time more wisely.

After RBCS preschoolers know the vowel and consonant sounds, alphabetical order is taught through singing "The Christ-Centered Alphabet Song." This song names each letter, its sound, and key Bible word corresponding with the *Christ-Centered Alphabet Wall Cards.* Spiritual truths once again are taught simultaneously with academics.

As attention spans increase, increase teaching periods accordingly. A general guideline is five minutes per year of age for each teaching session. This would mean that between twenty-four and thirty-six months of age, 10-minute sessions could be scheduled two or three times a day. Some toddlers can handle this in conjunction. In other words, some are so eager to learn that they prefer one twenty- to thirty-minute teaching period rather than several little ones. That teaching period could be split between phonics (sounds/symbols), number concepts 1-10, and phonics/math drill. (More on this later.)

CREATING A FUTURE WRITER

When your child seems ready, two areas which contribute toward future writing skills can also be added. For most toddlers, this can normally begin around age two or two-and-a-half.

My first recommendation is one which I wish every parent of a future RBCS kindergartner would practice prior to ever entrusting a child to our care. That is, *don't give a pencil to a toddler and just let him try writing letters on his own.* It is extremely difficult trying to undo bad printing habits. Therefore, some children never stop printing letters from bottom to top, right to left, upside down or backwards.

Printing utilizes fine motor skills. Running, hopping, climbing, jumping, and so forth are gross motor (large muscle) activities. Manipulatives like clay, puzzles, stacking/sorting, and cutting/pasting are fine motor (small muscle) activities which can facilitate development of our children's printing ability. Coloring large pictures can also foster the development of fine motor skills. But be sure to teach your child how to hold a crayon correctly.

By the end of their third year, most children are ready to begin learning to print. Printing can be learned best by starting out with a piece of chalk and a chalkboard. Gradually, work down to a sheet of plain paper and pencil, and then gradually convert to lined paper.

RBCS kindergartners first practice basic printing strokes. We call these the "big stick," "little stick," "lazy stick," "ball," and "hook." Combining these in one way or another will form most letters of the alphabet. The basic strokes are first practiced without lines. After a measure of printing success has been achieved without lines, we introduce lined paper.

BASIC STROKES

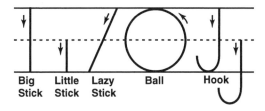

A highly effective method to introduce printing within lines is use of a green line on top, a dotted yellow line in the middle, and a red line on the bottom. We tell the children that these lines are like traffic lights. Green means "Go," yellow means "Caution," and red means "Stop." However, just as emergency vehicles have permission to break the law, there are some "lawbreaker" letters which go past the bottom red line (*g*, *j, p, q, y*). This technique helps them visualize placement better. Learning to print well takes time, practice, and patience.

Learning to write creatively also takes time, practice, and patience. But the desire to do so can be created early. In the beginning, this can be done by first helping your child think of a title for his "story."

Once such is decided, print the title for him, leaving a large enough space to draw a picture above the title when his story is finished. In a manner which makes the story his, thought processes should be guided to form several related short sentences.

Creating short stories is a wonderful opportunity to get children acquainted with "who, what, where, when, why, and how." Some children are a lot more adept at this than others. If there is not much success at first, try again a month or so later. Creative writing practices can also be motivational for learning to read and write independently.

These guidelines can encourage creativity plus build thinking skills. Teaching times should be enjoyable rather than "entertaining." Entertainment is Satan's counterfeit for joy. Learning itself should be made a JOY. Our own enthusiasm will go a long way toward creating such an atmosphere. The example we set should communicate that God wants us to LOVE learning, as a lifetime habit.

FILLING IN THE REMAINING TIME

Carrying out suggestions presented thus far involves only a portion of our children's day. What should we do with the remainder of their time?

The basic principle is that whatever we allow should in some measure be discipling them to hold the biblical world view, godly character, and academic skills necessary to fulfill God's calling and live for His glory.

This does not mean that every word spoken should be Scripture itself. That would be unrealistic.

It does mean, however, that thoughts, words, and deeds should be consistent with Scripture. Having Christ's mind in us (Phil 2:5), so that we can view every day activities as He would, comes from abiding in Him and His Word.

Let's apply that practically. From God's Word we learn of His delightful love for little children. Therefore, we can easily picture Him smiling approvingly as they try to climb their first tree, learn to swing, go up and down a slide "all by myself, Mommy!" giggle as they play in a lawn sprinkler, have water balloon "battles," "doggy" paddle in the water, attempt to throw and catch a ball, try to jump rope, or ride a tricycle. These and many other activities do not violate scriptural principles. Nor do they compete with our children's love for Christ. In fact, they complement that love as we teach them that every good gift and ability they have comes from Him!

Well-balanced days are vital to healthy development. This includes keeping a strong sense of humor, for "a merry heart does good like a medicine" (Prov 17:22). Seeing the funny side of life can mean "survival" in your family, as it did in ours. (All four of our grown children have tremendous wits and are passing on the same to their children!) Joyfulness is a matter of choice.

For example, catching a two-year-old running across the top of a neighbor's new Thunderbird, or finding him causing a neighborhood disturbance by perching on top of an eight-foot-high concrete fence barking at the dog next door, or hearing blood curdling yells while he's rolling down an incline into a briar patch (after being warned to stay off the fence!) can precipitate anger, anxiety (what will the neighbors think?), or a SMILE and a discipling moment.

Some of you may have suspected that the last few examples were from Randy's life. Gradually, I learned to take such moments in stride and keep smiling! (Except when spotting him at the top of a 40-foot pine tree! *Heart failure!*)

Even though at times Ed and I were tempted to pack all of our kids' lunches in road maps and say, "Write when you find work!" we hung in there and built many precious memories.

There are moments when we honestly can say, "These are the days which try Moms' souls. . . ." If you're like me, there are frustrating periods when the temptation to go hijack a pastry truck is very strong! And there are testings when the freight train of disappointment threatens to derail our faith. But this is all part of God's "well-balanced days," as He sends just the right doses of laughter and tears, victories and heartaches, and moments so precious with Him that words do not do them justice. This is the nature of the discipling process — in us first, and then instilled in our children. Keeping our eyes on that fact produces "strength made perfect in weakness" (2 Cor 12:9).

Carrying out discipleship includes staying alert to the pitfalls of television abuse and monitoring playtimes.

Television, sometimes called "the electronic babysitter," is one of Satan's greatest victories over reading, writing, and mastery of words. It is alarming to realize that in most homes, reports Phil Phillips, "sleeping is the only activity that children engage in more than watching television." Television can become physically addictive because it sends out electrodes to the brain which release a slight depressant. This is evidenced when children seem "glued" to the TV set.

TV addiction stimulates the right hemisphere of the brain (visual-spatial) while inhibiting the left hemisphere's (verbal-analytic) development. As a result, a child's analytical skills never fully develop. When that happens, he will have trouble learning on his own. Such children would rather passively "watch" than expend effort to acquire knowledge through reading. That leaves them open to attack by Satan and his forces.

Never Too Early

Consider this logic. Discerning truth from error requires finely honed thinking skills. Finely honed thinking skills require an extensive vocabulary. Reading is normally the main source for building such vocabulary. Those who fail to read extensively thus often never become independent thinkers. Those who cannot think are most likely to have their hearts and minds led astray by those who can.

Our children's souls are also at stake through certain commercial toys. Even the seemingly "cute and innocent" can have occult symbolisms behind their creation. As concerned parents, we need to be informed. Phil Phillips' book *Turmoil in the Toy Box* (Lancaster, PA: Starburst Publishers, 1986) is an eye-opener. This well-researched book deals with the dangers of television as well as many toys which have come on the market in recent years.[34]

Purchasing many toys is neither necessary nor desirable. Too many store-bought toys is poor financial stewardship. And they hamper creativity. Many enjoyable memories can be built from simple things like making tents out of sheets or blankets, playing with plastic bowls and utensils, building with boxes of all shapes and sizes, making dirt roads for little cars and trucks, preparing for motherhood with baby dolls, playing dress-up with discarded adult clothes and hats, observing and caring for God's creatures, playing store with empty products, and so on.

Play is an important learning medium. But we should be aware of what our children are doing to ensure that it is consistent with building disciples for Jesus.

A bonus is that as children build memories, they make some for us, too! Our Shari's adventure of helping her 85-year-old great-grandmother Becker mount Charlie for a pony ride created a precious photo memory. Lynda's amazement was comical when the photo she took of red ants turned out to reveal only our red clay road.

Randy's fascination with doodlebugs was a real surprise for me when I discovered them in piles of sand on his bookcase headboard! He explained that they were for "company" and observation, and that if he took them back outside they'd be "lonely."

Joey and Randy's "train" of canned goods from the kitchen through the living room into the bathroom made mealtimes "interesting" for several weeks. I had failed to notice when they started to remove the labels!

Lynda and Shari concluded recently that one of the best gifts we ever gave them was creativity. Since none of our children ever had many toys, this forced them to use their imaginations. All hold fond memories of creative ways they spent time together.

Their worktimes, caring for pets (two ponies, dogs, cats, birds) and play periods were balanced with academic pursuits. Each was taught faithfully about the Lord from birth on. Laying such a foundation was a precious privilege!

Is what has been shared in this chapter too lofty a goal to begin instilling in Christ's little lambs?

I think not. Through Christ, T. Van Der Kooy explains, "the soul of the child lays hold by intuition on many things which cannot be made clear to his intelligence. Especially must it be remembered that high and ideal thoughts facilitate and hasten the acquisition and the assimilation of subject matter that in many instances might be considered as lying beyond the comprehension of the child."[35] "For no other foundation can anyone lay than that which is laid, which is Jesus Christ" (1 Cor 3:11).

And we need to build upon that foundation faithfully.

Chapter Eight
Building on the Foundation: Three to Six

"All your children shall be taught by the Lord, And great shall be the peace of your children" (Isa 54:13).

"All your children shall be taught by the LORD, and great shall be the peace of your children," says **the Word**.

"By the year 2000 we will, I hope, raise our children to believe in human potential, not God."[36] This is the prevailing spirit in **the world**.

The battle for our children's souls is real!

We need a continuing plan for rearing our children to hold the biblical world view, godly character, and academic skills necessary to fulfill God's calling and live for His glory. Otherwise, our children are merely being raised (like cattle), not educated for God. They will therefore more likely follow the prevailing spirit of the world.

An architect must have a plan to build a solid structure. A surgeon must have a plan for successful surgery. A lawyer must have a plan to win a battle in court. So we must have a plan to win our children for Christ in the battle for their souls.

To be successful, an architect takes into account the stress factors of building materials. A surgeon must consider the stress factors of his patient. A lawyer has to be aware of the stress factors of his client.

So must we understand what constitutes ungodly stress and how to avoid it so our children will reach the educational goal for which they are being trained.

Stress, according to Webster's 1828 edition, means "force, violence, strain." As an educational example of stress, Webster listed Locke's view that "though the faculties of the mind are improved by exercise, yet they must not be put to a stress beyond their strength."

Forcing ("pushing") children's minds to strain beyond their abilities constitutes ungodly stress. This provokes them to exasperation (Eph 6:4), thus violating good pedagogy and God's law of love.

Improving the faculties of the mind by exercise, in accordance with God-given capabilities, is good for children, even though it involves applying pressure in their best interest.

Webster defines "pressure" as "a constraining force or impulse; that which urges or compels the intellectual or moral faculties; as the pressure of motives on the mind, or the fear on the conscience."

Reflect back to the meaning of "control," which is so necessary during the child stage (infancy to 12) of biblical child training. We learned that parents have the responsibility and legitimate right to control a child by exerting pressure which results from the restricting rules (standards) given to him for which he is then held accountable. This applies to the academic realm as well.

Genuine love will pay the price necessary to exercise our legitimate right to compel a child to use his God-given intellectual faculties. This type of pressure is godly because we know that it produces endurance which leads to proven character and unshakable confidence in Jesus Christ (Rom 5:3-5).

Because our generation has been brainwashed into thinking little children aren't "ready" for many things, the danger is that godly pressure can be misconstrued as "pushing." When that happens, we may back off and thereby shortchange God's heritage from receiving the quality of education He intends.

The best way I know to convey how much children between ages three and six are capable of handling, without "pushing," is to share what I have seen them achieve year after year at Rocky Bayou Christian School (RBCS).

THE ROCKY BAYOU CHRISTIAN SCHOOL KINDERGARTEN EXPERIENCE

RBCS began in 1973 with 22 students in Kindergarten through sixth grade. Five were kindergartners. In 1993, enrollment from three-year-old kindergarten through 12th exceeded 650; over 800 are anticipated for the 1994-95 school year.

As a result of faithfully seeking our Creator's wisdom concerning what His little ones can handle, this is what has been discovered since the fall of 1973.

Three-year-olds

According to how much time parents have spent talking to and reading with them, abilities and maturity levels vary widely in this age group. This is always taken into consideration.

In general, we have found that learning all the sounds of the short vowels and consonants plus reading one-vowel words by the end of the year is within reason. Knowing the letter names is also common.

One gifted three-year-old read the Childcraft® encyclopedias (published by World Book, Inc.) by the end of her first year. Several others learned the alphabet sounds within a week and quickly "took off" in a reader. But most take three to six months before they are ready to begin a short-vowel reader. A few are not ready until the four-year-old program the next fall. (Keep in mind that these are children who normally had no prior teaching.)

In math, three-year-olds (*threes*) well handle counting to 100 by 1s, 10s, and 5s. They can be introduced to the number sequence 0–100 and can achieve a good grasp of concepts ("how many"), at least through 10. In addition, threes can comprehend the concept of addition facts through the five combinations. For example, it is easy for them to concretely figure out that "3 apples + 2 apples = 5 apples."

Time factors to accomplish these results amount to 15 minutes each for phonics and math. A 10-15 minute phonics/math drill is also conducted later in the morning. The remainder of their morning consists of Bible, large/fine motor skills development activities, snack/recess, vocabulary development, art or music, free play, and story/poetry/sharing times.

By the second semester of school (late January), if a class is able, brief seatwork periods are included for phonics/math. Usually, this involves about 1/2 sheet for each subject. These are very simple exercises, easily prepared by a teacher or parent. (No workbooks are used for threes.) If a few are not yet ready to print, they are occupied constructively while the others press on.

It warms my heart every time I visit a K3 class! What a wondrous experience to watch spiritual, moral, and academic seeds being sown in their budding little hearts and minds! These precious little ones respond beautifully to a loving yet disciplined atmosphere.

Four-year-olds

Fours are delightful! Though lots of mothering is still in order, their minds are eager to learn "like the big kids." Fours commonly achieve a first grade level in phonics, reading, and math.

Consider what they are capable of learning in phonics alone: short/long vowels, consonants, ending consonant blends, consonant digraphs, consonant blends, plus naming and describing words. They also drill the letter names/sounds for the vowel digraphs, modified vowels, and diphthongs to enable capable students to grow in their reading skills.

In addition to learning sound/symbol relationships, spelling rules build their thinking skills. Printing abilities are usually proficient by second semester.

Unless there has been a diagnosed learning disability, which have been few in number, I have never seen a properly taught four-year-old who was unable to read at least one syllable words. Because phonics is so easy, if a child fails to read by spring, he or she is recommended for testing. Usually, the diagnosis has been either an auditory or visual perception problem. Identifying the problem early enables us through remedial instruction to help prevent a harmful build-up of "feelings of failure."

In math, fours are also amazing. Counting by 1s, 10s, 5s, and 2s to 100 is a breeze. So is recognizing and writing numbers 0–100. Gaining a fairly good grasp of the concept "how many" to 100 is not difficult either. We continually use concrete methods ("hands on") followed by semi-abstract (pictured objects) and then abstract teaching (numbers and facts only).

Learning the addition/subtraction combinations through 10 has consistently resulted in performing 50 addition facts in 1-3 minutes and 50 subtraction facts in 3-5 minutes.

Phonics/math teaching periods last about 45 minutes total. However, time is allotted for "wiggle breaks." Because teaching changes content every 5 minutes or so, attention is easily maintained. Phonics/math seatwork periods also take about 45 minutes. (More on this in a moment.) Singing to the Lord at key points breaks up the seatwork period, refreshes spirits/bodies, and heightens interest.

The remainder of the morning consists of Bible, snack/recess, phonics/math drill, vocabulary development, art or music, free play, and story/poetry/sharing times.

Every time I witness four-year-olds in a learning session, I can't help but praise God for the abilities He has given such little ones! And hearts are so tender toward the Lord at this age. In fact, many receive Him as personal Savior before the year is out. Their spiritual perceptivity is marvelous to behold!

Five-year-olds

This age group is impressive, to say the least! During this time, the last of their peak formative years, potential for spiritual, moral, and academic growth is astounding. Achieving a second to third grade level in phonics, reading, and math is not uncommon.

In addition to the material fours cover in phonics/spelling, fives also learn how to add suffixes *s*, *es*, *ed*, and *ing*, plus the phonics/spelling rules for vowel digraphs, modified vowels, and diphthongs. In addition, they study syllabication and accent rules for reading multi-syllabled words. They drill the variant (not fitting normal patterns) vowel sounds, variant consonant sounds, plus silent consonants. Students at this age can easily apply their growing knowledge of nouns, verbs, and adjectives to identifying the "who," "doing," and "what" of sentences (subject/predicate). Writing short stories is enjoyed as well.

As mentioned previously, it is common for a five-year-old to be able to locate any passage in Scripture quickly and read it with proficiency. But don't just take my word for it. Listen to what Dr. Jay Grimstead, Director of Coalition on Revival (C.O.R.), has to say:

> *When I visited RBCS where Doreen Claggett's breathtaking early curriculum and pedagogy were applied to children starting at age three, I was pleasantly shocked.*

> The school's director, Col. Bob Grete, had two
> five-year-olds (one black and one white) come over
> and let me quiz them on theological questions and
> Bible reading. They instantly and confidently found
> and read accurately any Scripture passages I asked
> of them, then answered questions about the Trinity
> and two natures of Christ which would have pleased
> Athanasius.
>
> Since that day I have been proclaiming the
> courageous educational breakthrough on total
> worldview education that is happening through
> Mrs. Claggett's biblical world view curriculum and
> methodology.

What can fives accomplish in math? They can count by 1s, 10s, 5s, 2s, 3s, and 4s to 100+, as well as write numbers to 999. Understanding number concepts is accomplished through "hands on" activities plus place value instruction for 1s, 10s, and 100s places. Five-year-olds proficiently accomplish 50 addition/subtraction combinations through the teens in less than five minutes. Learning two- and three-digit addition/subtraction plus greater-than/less-than comparisons through 999 is learned with ease. So is instruction on fractions (1/2, 1/3, 1/4), time (hour, 1/2 hour, 1/4 hour) and money (pennies, nickels, dimes, quarters, half-dollars).

Phonics/reading/math instruction plus seatwork takes about two hours per day. (Less time is spent covering the same material in a home school environment.) Originally, RBCS had only a half-day program for K5 classes. However, as enrollment grew, with it grew the number of five-year-old non-nappers who were staying all day. Therefore, to be better stewards of their time with us, the program was expanded to a full day (8:15-3:15).

The remainder of the morning is spent on Bible, phonics/math drill and a snack/recess. After lunch is a relaxed period for either history or science, art or music, story time and physical education.

Seeds sown in the threes, sprout in the fours, and come into bloom in the fives. These precious little children are already becoming beautiful works of art, created in Christ Jesus for His honor and glory!

Letting such tender plants grow "freely," as Froebel advocated, subjects them to the choking weeds of worldliness. Nurturing in the greenhouse of God's love and discipline until their roots go down deep, thereby being strengthened to withstand the harsh elements of the world, is the key to equipping them for every good work (Psa 1:3, 2 Tim 3:17). Envision that potential as they continue to be discipled to remember their Creator in the days of their youth (Eccl 12:1)!

RBCS Kindergarten Results

As measured by the 1970 California Achievement Test (CAT) designed for first graders, K5 classes with one year's education have traditionally averaged a median Grade Equivalent (G.E.) score of 2.25 with a median Percentile of 86.4. K5s having had two years' education have averaged a 3.02 median G.E. and a median Percentile of 98.8.

Kindergarten graduates consistently maintain above-grade-level performance. For example, by the end of fourth grade, one group scored a median G.E. of 7.4, with 5.6 the lowest and 10.6 the highest scores. Another group, at the end of fifth grade scored a median G.E. of 8.5, with the lowest score being 6.3 and the highest 11.2. A third group by the end of sixth grade scored a median G.E. of 9.9. Two original kindergartners graduated from RBCS in 1987. By ninth grade, both maxed the CAT with a 13.6 G.E. and Percentiles of 97 and 92.

RBCS Superintendent Bob Grete has found that former kindergartners hold the highest degree of thinking skills and have therefore been his best students in the upper grades.

Katherine Grete, RBCS elementary grades supervisor and director of Talent Development (a program designed for learning disabled students) has also reported that kindergarten graduates are by far more competent, both academically and in character, than those joining such students at higher grade levels.

Such results are the outcome of a deep sense of stewardship: "Moreover it is required in stewards that one be found faithful" (1 Cor 4:2).

In both home and Christian school, every moment should be taken captive for Christ (2 Cor 10:3-5). For each of us will one day give an account of how we have handled that stewardship responsibility (Rom 14:12).

Understanding and applying the principle of the talents (Matt 25:14-29) is at the heart of exercising wise stewardship over our children's development. Regardless of whether God has given one, five, or ten talents, those talents are to be multiplied for our Master's use. This calls for an active investment of time and energy on our part as well as the children's. (If this effort is not made, the "use it or lose it" principle applies.)

A basic teaching principle is that each child should be held accountable only for what he is capable of doing, not what another child can do. In other words, we should not compare one child with another, but gently challenge each to give his very best for God. The Lord asks no more than that; neither should we.

BUILDING GODLY CHARACTER
THROUGH SEATWORK

Seatwork sessions present wonderful opportunities to encourage the faithful development of individual abilities. (More on biblically teaching subjects will be presented later.)

"Seatwork" is a term referring to working on phonics/ spelling/penmanship/math exercises. In Webster's 1828 dictionary, the closest definition for "seatwork" is "that which is performed by mental labor." The pressure of causing children to exert their mental faculties is a necessary part of God's lesson plan for their growth to Christian maturity.

With both K4 and K5 classes, RBCS uses the *Christ-Centered Phonics* and *Christ-Centered Math Workbooks*. These workbooks contain exercises which teach children's spirits while effectively enabling a teacher to individually evaluate academic understanding. Pacing needs are adjusted as each class progresses, speeding up or slowing down accordingly. Doing all things decently and in order (1 Cor 14:40) is a primary requirement for teachers and students alike. Christ's mind cannot be taught well in a disorderly environment where children are in control rather than the teacher. Once biblical standards for conduct are set, God expects us to lovingly enforce those standards.

For example, training children to follow instructions as asked, whether they feel like doing so or not, disciplines them to understand that when we "lose" self, we "win" in character. (To let a child ignore instructions would be training in disobedience.)

By the manner in which children perform their seatwork tasks, they are forming habits as patterns for other areas of life. Therefore, one character builder is teaching children to work quickly, therefore learning to "redeem the time" by using it wisely (Eph 5:15-16). If not corrected when they are little, a lifetime habit of being "poky" can develop. We have all seen adults who seem to move in slow motion. Some of this may be attributable to temperament, but in many cases it is a result of poor training when little.

"He who is faithful in what is least is faithful also in much" (Luke 16:10) includes discipling children to persevere when things seem hard. Giving up rather than expending effort is always easier. This is the time to apply godly pressure rather than let a child form the habit of quitting. By doing so, sooner or later will come the discovery that perseverance is its own reward. Consider little Joanne's experience as a classic example.

"Joanne, because I love you I'm not going to let you give up. Let's ask the Lord together to help you, and He will," I reassured. Joanne stands out in my mind because of her reaction after struggling for several weeks with addition facts sheets. When she finally "got it" by accomplishing 50 facts perfectly in less than three minutes, with a beaming face she exclaimed, "Aren't I terrific!?" She did fine thereafter, having learned a very valuable lesson in perseverance. Perseverance is the key to achieving the quality each child is capable of giving.

"Whatever your hand finds to do, do it with thy might" (Eccl 9:10) is a strong motivator to do the finest job possible for the Lord, even down to the smallest details. For our great God is a God of detail (Luke 12:7).

His attention to detail and its perfection can be seen in all of creation. He therefore even cares about the manner in which we print characters such as letters and numbers.

The word "character" has an external and internal meaning. Externally, the word "character" refers to "letters," "the manner of writing," or "distinctive quality of any kind strongly marked." Internally, "character" refers to distinctive aspects of character or reputation. As we learn the identification and reproduction of individual letters, we are also imprinting the mark of Christian character on our lives.

Because of this, we teach students by example to reflect Christ's character in penmanship. They are discipled to accept stewardship of the ability to use a pencil with excellence for the glory of God. (This also involves exercising stewardship over the care of supplies plus making restitution for carelessness or purposeful destruction.)

We have a saying at RBCS: "Messy doesn't count." This means that if a child is done quickly but his work is messy, it does not "count" and he is asked to do it over. Quality should not be sacrificed for quantity. Without quality, time, resources, and talents are being wasted. Therefore, as each child's printing skills improve, he is held accountable for working at that new level of performance.

As kindergartners become more and more proficient, we carefully guard against their becoming "puffed up." Because talents are God's gifts, the child who uses five or ten talents well is given no greater praise than the one with lesser abilities who is also doing his best. For the Lord hates a proud heart (Prov 6:16, 16:18).

Rather than taking the credit themselves, we make every effort to train children to thank their Creator for whatever abilities they have. Using those abilities for Him is simply God's "just due." Even little children need to understand and apply this principle: "Let another man praise you, and not your own mouth; a stranger, and not your own lips" (Prov 27:2).

On this same subject, we avoid the overuse of rewards which can contribute to pridefulness. A child who always has stickers, stars, happy faces, and so forth on his papers can easily become "puffed up." Even worse, he can be trained to expect a reward for everything he does! Or, he might become arrogant and critical of other children who don't receive as many.

Children should be taught to do what is right *because* it is right, not for what they may get out of it. They need to learn to work "as to the Lord and not to men" (Eph 6:6-7). Verbal encouragement plus an occasional sticker, star, or "happy face" is certainly a good motivator. But this technique is used sparingly, with sensitivity to any negative character traits which may develop as a result.

Averting the build-up of pride requires that the child with five or ten talents not be permitted to be critical of another with lesser abilities. This spirit is God's desire for adults and children alike: "Put on tender mercies, kindness, humility, meekness, longsuffering . . ." (Col 3:12). Students who finish assignments early are taught that they have an opportunity to practice God's law of love by not disturbing those still working. This principle is applicable: "aspire to lead a quiet life, to mind your own business, and to work with your own hands . . ." (1 Thess 4:11). Working "with your own hands" requires that cheating (for example, stealing answers or letting someone else steal answers) be curbed right from the beginning. The principle is this: "Let him who stole steal no longer, but rather let him labor, working with his hands that which is good . . ." (Eph 4:28).

Letting someone cheat is unloving because it robs him of an opportunity to learn. Stealing someone else's answers is also deceitful because it is lying by making the teacher think the child did the work himself.

Occasionally, a kindergarten teacher or parent may be confronted with cries of "I can't do it!" This, too, is often a form of lying due to laziness. Or, when after being asked a question, a child responds with a shrug of the shoulder and a whining statement like, "I don't know . . ." In reality, it may very well be a cover-up lie for "I don't want to tell you . . ." rather than a lack of knowledge.

Such behavior exemplifies the hypocrisy I spoke about earlier. Remember, children will do whatever bad (or even good) it takes to get their own way. Lying is to be put away and truth spoken to every person, for "we are members of one another" (Eph 4:25). This brings me to a very important point, Mom.

". . . We should no longer be children, tossed to and fro and carried about with every wind of doctrine, by the trickery of men, in the cunning craftiness of deceitful plotting, but, speaking the truth in love, may grow up in all things into Him who is the head — Christ . . ." (Eph 4:14-15).

The truth is, beloved, that in spite of the fine results schools like RBCS can achieve, you, as a dedicated mother, can do an even better job!

The discipling I've been talking about during seatwork sessions especially is like standing at the window to a child's heart. These periods represent teaching moments in which each child's character flaws are likely to surface. The flesh does not like accountability. Consider how Adam and Eve tried to sidestep that issue in the Garden of Eden! Applying the godly pressure of accountability enables the one teaching to "see" into a child's carnal nature and deal with it biblically. And you, if there is any way possible to do so, are the best person to be standing at that "window."

Standing at "the window" in the home provides the highest degree of continuity in applying "Thus says the Lord." And it has been proven that a tutorial situation is far more productive than a class environment. Home schooling is both a high calling and a marvelous challenge. However, continuing success comes through being aware ahead of time that it will not always be easy. Nothing worthwhile ever is.

A friend of mine, Dr. James Truax, likens this to the tide rolling in and out. As formal home schooling first begins, often everything appears beautiful, as when the tide is in at the beach and gentle waves are lapping the seashore. However, as the tide goes out at that shore, the garbage hidden underneath begins to surface (for instance, dead fish, broken shells, seaweed, trash dumped overboard from boats).

So it is in the tide of home schooling. Increasing expectations and godly pressures cause garbage like laziness, pridefulness, rebellion, procrastination, lying, sloppiness, willfulness, foolishness, forgetfulness, carelessness, etc. to surface. The nature and amount of garbage will vary from child to child, but this is good, not bad. The Lord wants "godly offspring" (Mal 2:15). Therefore the tide in/tide out process is His way of purifying His children.

When character flaws begin to surface, remaining alert to Satan's darts is vital. Because a child's heart usually mirrors that of his primary teachers, (his parents [Luke 6:40]), "window" moments can prompt a surfacing of our own character flaws. If not dealt with biblically, a cycle can be created which may lead to a wrongful conclusion that the problem is home schooling or "too early education." And that is exactly what God's arch-enemy (and ours) wants.

Bailing out or becoming discouraged is Satan's goal. Choosing to rejoice in the privilege of cleaning up the garbage in our children's lives as well as our own is God's way. As "self" rears its ugly head, by God's grace, we can deck it! All such teaching moments are wonderful opportunities to further disciple and be discipled for Christ. If your children are sent outside the home to be taught, you forfeit your right to see your own nature. In that sense, as Dr. Truax likes to say, "Home schooling is even more a parent training than child training movement!"

PUTTING PHONICS/MATH DRILLS AND GAMES IN PROPER PERSPECTIVE

For some, part of "parent training" is to be educated regarding the value of rote memorization plus discerning legitimate games from harmful ones.

Adults often think that drill is boring, so naturally, children must also hate drills. On the contrary. Most children enjoy repetition. It gives them a sense of accomplishment to recite rhymes, verses, letter names/sounds/key words, math facts, and so on.

Memorization exercises the brain so that memorization becomes easier and easier. (This pays off when memorizing God's Word.) Regular phonics/math drills are a vital part of a young child's learning process. Drill content represents more "coat hangers for the future," which sooner or later will all be hung in their right closets.

For example, from the first day of instruction, in echo style, RBCS kindergartners begin drilling "*Aa* says /ă/ in

Adam; *Bb* says /b/ in Bible; *Cc* says /k/ in commands," and so forth through "*Zz* says /z/ in Zaccheus." It matters not whether the children understand this information. As the teacher proceeds with her lessons, she puts meaning to the drill and it soon makes sense.

Drilling ahead of the actual instruction benefits both the advanced children and less mature. The less mature need plenty of repetition. The more advanced quickly pick up on the sounds, learn to blend, and are soon ready to start in a reader. Individualized reading programs allow each to proceed without some being held back and others "pushed."

This same principle is applied in math. For instance, addition/subtraction facts are drilled long before students are taught the concepts. Already familiar with the facts, when the practical application begins, the learning process becomes easier.

Drill periods are kept enjoyable as well as instructive. However, we do lovingly hold the children to the principle that there is a time to speak, and a time to keep silence (Eccl 3:7). Therefore, they speak together in unison during drill periods. None are permitted to blurt out answers or rush ahead of the others. For this is often a manifestation of pride. It also produces confusion, and God is not the author of confusion (1 Cor 14:33).

Variety helps maintain enthusiasm. As does utilization of drill techniques which involve physical activity whenever possible. For example, drilling Phonics Section I (*Aa* to *Zz*) is often conducted in this manner. While students are in a seated position, the teacher drills rhythmically, "*Aa* says /ă/ in Adam. **What** says /ă/ in Adam?" The children quickly stand and respond in rhythm, "**Aa** says /ă/ in Adam." In turn the teacher asks, "*Aa* says **what** in Adam?" The children respond with, "*Aa* says **/ă/** in Adam." Students are up and down throughout this procedure.

On another occasion, a Jack-in-a-Box drill might be used. Students squat in an orderly fashion and then gleefully "pop" out of their boxes to echo the teacher's drill. On other days a slow drill/fast drill method works best, as might singing particular parts like the blends (for example, /să/, /sĕ/, /sĭ/, /sŏ/, /sŭ/). Sometimes we alternate between "girls only" and "boys only." Even though the content is fairly routine, the manner in which drills are conducted varies from day to day.

Math drills especially lend themselves to activity. Counting by 1s is often done with calisthenics, or marching around the room (perhaps like a train and tooting "horns" on the 10s). When counting by 5s, children enjoy standing on the 5s count and sitting on the 10s. Clapping as they count by 10s is also enjoyed.

One technique for drilling math facts is playing "Around the World." To play this game, students stand next to their seats. A designated child comes and stands beside another. The teacher flashes a math fact, and the two race to see who can identify the sum or difference the fastest. The winner moves on to stand beside the next student, and so forth. This type of game focuses upon the objective (learning the math facts), not the means (the game itself). Therefore, it is a legitimate biblical method.

Biblical methodology requires that every moment be taken captive for Christ. The use of puppets and games in the classroom is an area in which I have learned to be cautious. So much of what is used in our nation's classrooms has a "fun, fun, fun" emphasis which fosters a please-me-ism mentality.

I used to use puppets and fun games myself until two events occurred. The first was a visit to RBCS by a traveling evangelism team which used puppets to teach the gospel. Students in kindergarten through sixth grade attended their presentation. It was indeed entertaining, for students and teachers alike. And it was obvious that the evangelism team genuinely loved the Lord.

The problem revealed itself the next day. All the teachers through sixth grade quizzed their students about the presentation. We were curious about what the children remembered. The results were unanimous. The students remembered the cute puppets; none recalled the message.

The second eye-opener occurred shortly thereafter. During the months my mother and father were both dying, I did not have time to prepare the "extras" for my lessons as usual. So I just taught. After about two months of this, one morning a "light" went on in my mind. It was as if the Lord were saying, "Doreen, look carefully at these fours. They are excited about learning itself! And you have not been using your fun techniques for quite some time!"

From my first moment of teaching, I have always sought to lift up the Lord before my students. But I had still fallen into the entertainment trap. "After all," I reasoned, "shouldn't schooling be as enjoyable as possible?" To brainwashed minds, however, "enjoyable" is normally equated with "fun" rather than with its root "joy." Fun focuses on self-pleasure; joy or delight is found in the Lord (Neh 8:10). Rearing godly children who love to learn is an outgrowth of fostering delight in God and studying while still little.

KEEPING THE RIGHT FOCUS

Gregg Harris, director of Christian Life Workshops and author of *The Christian Home School*, explains:

> . . . The idea of study being motivated by delight is shown in Psalm 111:2, "Great are the words of the Lord; they are pondered by all who delight in them." Psalm 37:4 implies that when we are delighted in the Lord, He will instill proper desires in our hearts and then satisfy them.

He continues by sharing these insights for parents:

> In delight-directed learning, the companion-teacher/parent demonstrates his wisdom and his delight in learning to his children by his life and

> *activities. He involves his children in these activities as much as possible in order to pass on to them his wisdom as well as his tastes, interests, and desires. Then he designs study projects that use these interests as motivation for developing skills and gaining knowledge in other areas.*[37]

Being responsive to our children's needs as their tastes and interests begin to form can develop both godly character and a delight in studying.

For example, at age three, our Shari visited her great uncle's horse ranch. (She still remembers the crazy horse that stuck out his tongue to be petted. The more she petted its tongue, the further he stuck it out!) Ever since, she has had a passion for horses.

As an early reader, she read everything she could get her hands on about horses (for instance, fiction stories, Christian biographies of people who had horses, medical reports, training manuals). She learned so much by age eight that when she got her first pony (a miraculous answer to her prayers!), we relied on her to tell us what care Charlie needed.

Shari learned responsibility by applying: "A righteous man regards the life of his animal" (Prov 12:10). Practical application of math was gained through learning about the expenses involved in Charlie's care and feeding. Biblical parent/child training principles were acquired through relating those to her frustration over his occasional stubborn refusal to obey her training commands.

She learned how to compete God's way at horse shows, how to win — or lose — with a right attitude. Leadership skills were acquired through service in a "4H Club." Her interest in horses was even reflected in what she did in art (and at times music). In fact, we used to tease her that before she'd let a man marry her, he would have to agree with: "Love me; love my horse!" (As it turned out, her husband, Mark, is into computers — not horses.)

Academically, Shari excelled. At age six, she completed first grade, second, and half of third. She maintained that lead throughout school, graduating at age 16 as her class's Most Outstanding Student. Giving her a genuinely Christian education, plus using her natural interest to relate everything to "Thus says the Lord," combined to make her into the godly young woman she is today.

Yet, this is but a shadow of what can be accomplished through godly parents committed to home schooling.

A delight-directed approach combines both learning and doing from a child's earliest years, as did our Hebrew and Christian forefathers before us. The goal is not to give children a high school education by the time they are out of elementary school, but to begin while the bulk of their character is still forming to develop godly habits and attitudes toward study which will last a lifetime.

Children three to six should be taught as long as in the process we don't destroy their natural desire to learn. Their God-given eagerness to learn "like the big kids" is a springboard for showing them not only *how* to study, but also find delight in doing so. If we do this right, even work can seem like play to our children.

Doing it right begins with teaching children's spirits and trusting God to open their intellects.

Chapter Nine

Revealing God
Through Reading and Math

※⚙❀⚙❀

"Blessed is he who reads and those who hear . . .
and keep those things which are written in it . . ."
(Rev 1:3).

Teaching infants the mother tongue is perhaps the most difficult task of all education. Yet, we moms do this with ease. Therefore, nurturing children's spirits while teaching them to read is well within grasp.

God holds a high view of reading. Using a *Strong's Concordance*, a profitable exercise would be to look up scriptural references for "read," "readest," "readeth," and "reading." In doing so, you will find that the act of reading God's Word is almost always accompanied by an exhortation to hear and apply what is read. This represents the three levels of reading.

A biblical example is found in Revelation 1:3: "Blessed is he who reads and those who hear . . . and keep those things which are written in it. . . ." The word "reads" is the first level, which involves the mechanics of reading. At the reception level, the reader is going through the mechanics of pronouncing words.

To "hear" the words means that they now take on meaning. At this second level, the reader comprehends the idea the Author is trying to communicate.

The highest level of reading is application. This means understanding why the idea was given in the first place, how God wants to change lives through it, then following through with action to "keep" what is required. Thus, the reader becomes not only a hearer but a doer of the Word.

Philip's encounter with the Ethiopian eunuch is a practical illustration of all three levels of reading. Particularly applicable verses from Acts 8:29-37 are as follows:

> *Then the Spirit said to Philip, "Go near and overtake this chariot." So Philip ran to him, and heard him reading the prophet Isaiah, and said, "Do you understand what you are reading?" And he said, "How can I, unless someone guides me?"*

"Do you understand what you are reading?" illustrates God's view on the importance of reading for meaning. **"How can I, unless someone guides me?"** indicates that having the phonetic tools alone is not enough for competent reading comprehension and thus application. The eunuch was already capable of reading the passage, but he lacked sufficient skills to comprehend its meaning. He needed further guidance to move from the first to the second level of reading so that he could understand the ideas that the words were expressing.

Once Philip helped the eunuch comprehend what he was reading, the eunuch quickly moved to apply what he had read, which is the third level of reading. He demonstrated that he was moved to action when he believed on Christ and asked to be baptized (vs. 36-37). At this highest level of reading, he was now able to see why the ideas in the Scripture passage were given in the first place and how God meant to change his life through that message.

For our children to fruitfully read, comprehend, and obey Scripture, they need phonetic tools, reading comprehension skills, and discernment to rightly apply whatever is read.

"Discernment" in Webster's 1828 edition is "the power or faculty of the mind, by which it distinguishes one thing from another, as truth from falsehood; virtue from vice; acuteness of judgment; power of perceiving differences in things or ideas, and their relations and tendencies. The errors of youth often proceed from the want of discernment."

The ability to discern truth from falsehood; virtue from vice in reading materials comes from knowing the Truth, which is "a discerner of the thoughts and intents of the heart" (Heb 4:12). Therefore, we ought to nurture children's spirits as they are acquiring the phonetic tools necessary for reading. Revealing God's Word and His ways through the medium of reading should eventually produce the discernment necessary to perceive truth from error when later faced with a broad variety of reading materials.

The best way I know to further explain how to disciple children's spirits while teaching the mechanics of reading is to share some examples of how Rocky Bayou Christian School teachers first introduce students to phonics. (Thousands of home schooling families, as well as other Christian schools, are also using the same system and God is richly blessing.)

FIRST LEVEL OF READING

The selected examples were taken from the *Aa*–**Adam lesson** in the *Christ-Centered Phonics Lessons for Flashcards 1–31* (Christ Centered Publications, 1992). These exercises (plus a few not mentioned) would be spread over three or four days, with teaching times lasting about 15–20 minutes each.

PHONICS DRILL INTRODUCTION: The teacher holds up Cards 1–31 of the colorfully illustrated *Christ-Centered Phonics Flashcards Set* and says: "In my hand are cards which represent the 26 letters of our English alphabet — five vowels plus 21 consonants. Jesus Christ, our Creator, gave us the alphabet as a foundation for words. Words are His way to tell us all about Himself. Words give us the ability to better know God and to make Him known. That is why we need to learn all the letters of the alphabet, the sounds they make, and how to blend those sounds together to read words. This will help you learn to read God's Word, the Bible. It is through God's Word that He speaks to us and shows us His truth about everything in life. Nothing is more important to learn than God's truth!

"We'll now begin the exciting adventure of learning to read by saying the letter names, sounds, and key words for the alphabet. I will say them first, and then you may have a turn." The teacher proceeds through each card in this format: "Short *Aa* says /ă/ in Adam; *Bb* says /b/ in Bible, *Cc* says /k/ in commands, and so forth, through *Zz* says /z/ in Zaccheus."

The drill session continues for a few minutes with several other simple drills. Because drill content is always in advance of associated lessons, this allows each child to proceed at his own pace. Reading lessons are individualized. Each student begins a reader as soon as he learns the alphabet sounds, can blend an initial consonant and a vowel together, and then add an ending consonant sound.

CARD 1 INTRODUCTION: On Day Two of the lesson, the teacher reviews the spiritual application on the **Aa–Adam card** by saying: "Let's learn a little more about the meaning of the picture on Card 1. God's Word says, '. . . it is written, The first man Adam was made a living soul; the last Adam was made a quickening spirit. The first man is of earth, earthy: the second man is the Lord from heaven. And as we have born the image of the earthy, we shall also bear the image of the heavenly' (1 Cor 15:45, 47-49). In that passage, God is telling us that the man Adam failed to pass God's test of obedience for us. However, Jesus Christ, who is called the 'last Adam,' had no sin and therefore passed God's obedience test perfectly for us. Therefore, God the Father accepted Christ's death on the cross as punishment for our sins.

"We are born in Adam's likeness in that we have his same sin nature. Unless we ask Jesus to be our Lord and Savior, we will always be like Adam. However, when we ask Jesus to be our Lord and Savior, then we are born from above, with a new nature. As we get to know Jesus better, we will thus more and more want to please Him instead of ourselves."

On Day Three, holding the **Aa-Adam card**, she introduces the upper/lower case *Aa* by saying: "Because God is a God of order, He has given us many rules to live by. He even has rules for the use of letters. The capital letter, like the big *A* (she points to the *A* on Card 1), is used at the beginning of sentences. A sentence is a complete thought. For example, if I said to you, 'Adam gave the . . . ,' would only those words be a complete thought which made sense? Now, consider this statement: 'Adam gave the animals names.' That would make the thought complete, wouldn't it? God expects us to use words in orderly, complete thoughts.

"Another rule for letters is that we need to use a capital letter at the beginning of special words like people's names. Adam's name begins with a capital *A*. (She writes 'Adam' on the board and underlines the *A*.) Small letters are used when capitals aren't needed. A small *a* (she points to the *a* on Card 1) is at the beginning of the word 'animals.'" (She writes "animals" and underlines the *a*.)

She continues by saying, "Before Adam sinned and had to leave the beautiful garden, God talked with Adam often. God even asked Adam to give names to the animals. I wonder what Adam thought about all the different sounds the animals made! For example, what sound would he have heard a cat make? A hen? A pig? A dog? A duck?

"We can hear the sounds animals make, but we can't understand what they mean. That is because God only gave people the ability to speak in meaningful sounds. We call meaningful sounds words. The orderly arrangement of sounds produces words with meaning. Each letter in the alphabet has a particular sound, just as animals have a particular sound." At this point, the "Noah's Vowel Song," mentioned in Chapter Seven, is introduced.

AUDITORY DISCRIMINATION: Auditory discrimination is the ability to distinguish one sound from another. This is the first step in phonics training. Here is an example of one type of listening exercise. The teacher holds up Card 1 and says: "The sentences I'm going to read contain some words which begin with the /ă/ sound like we hear at the beginning of Adam's name. You need very good 'listening ears' to find the words! First, close your eyes. Then, when you hear a word beginning with /ă/, let me know by raising your hand. Ready? (The teacher slightly emphasizes the underlined words below as she reads.)

"'<u>After</u> sin entered the world through <u>Adam's</u> disobedience, people born thereafter had hearts that naturally wanted to do wrong. But when we <u>ask</u> Jesus to be our Savior, He forgives our sin <u>and</u> gives us a clean heart — one which then wants to do right! How wonderful!'"

VISUAL DISCRIMINATION: Visual discrimination is the ability to distinguish one letter or group of letters from others. The teacher uses a laminated figure of a boy holding a magnifying glass plus laminated outlines of footprints. Before this exercise, she writes specific letters on the footprints with a dry erase pen, then says: "When we ask Jesus to forgive us and be our Savior, He gives us a clean heart — one which then wants to do right! How can you know if I'm really telling the truth? You can be like the Bereans in Scripture who 'received the word with all readiness of mind, and searched the scriptures daily, whether those things were so' (Acts 17:11). That word 'searched' means 'to examine or investigate.' Have you ever seen a magnifying glass like the one in this picture? (She attaches the figure of the boy/magnifying glass picture to the chalkboard.) A magnifying glass makes it possible to search or investigate the tiniest details of something not easily seen with just our eyes.

In much the same way, the Bereans didn't trust their own view of something. Instead, because they understood that God's Word is truth (John 17:17), they used the lens of Scripture to search out right from wrong regarding even the tiniest of teachings. As they read the Scriptures, God the Holy Spirit gladly taught them how to follow in Christ's footsteps by always doing those things which please Father God (1 Pet 2:21, John 8:29).

"The picture of the boy and magnifying glass, plus these footprints (she now places the footprints on the board), can remind us that we also need to learn how to search the Scriptures daily so that the Holy Spirit can teach us right from wrong. It pleases God the Father when we obediently seek to follow in His Son's footsteps. Before we are ready to search the Scriptures, however, we must be able to read well. We begin by learning the alphabet letter names and their sounds." The lesson continues by asking a student to remove any footprints that do not contain the letter that stands for the short *Aa* sound.

This exercise is gradually expanded to having students identify particular blends or words. Later on, the footprints will contain words that need to be put in "sentence order." By that time, the nature of the instructions fosters thinking skills.

Another very important visual discrimination exercise is "Jacob's Phonics Ladder" (a laminated chart picturing a ladder with a Shekinah glory cloud illustration at the top). This visual aid teaches a sequence of specific reading skills which culminates in learning syllabication and accent rules at the advanced level. The ladder is introduced by holding up the ladder and saying: "Do you remember the Bible account of Jacob's special dream? (See Genesis 28:10-22.) In that dream, Jacob saw a ladder whose parts touched both heaven and earth. Angels were going up and down that ladder. At the very top was Jehovah, the God of Abraham, Isaac, and Jacob, who appeared in the form of the Shekinah glory cloud. God, the Word, spoke to

Jacob out of that cloud. He promised great blessings to Jacob. In return, Jacob promised to serve God all the days of his life, and to give back to God a tenth of whatever He gave to Jacob. Because of all that God has done for us as well, we should also want to love and serve Him — just like Jacob did!"

"At the top of this phonics ladder is an illustration (point to the Shekinah glory cloud) which reminds us of God's bright glory, and that it was Jesus, the Word, Jehovah the Son, who spoke from the Shekinah. In the written Word, the Bible, God reveals His greatest blessings to us! To be able to receive those blessings, we need to be able to read. The first step in learning to read is to learn the letter names and their sounds. On the ladder I've written the vowels, which are the first letters we'll be studying. Let's go over their short sounds now." The teacher and students then go over the sounds together.

Related Phonics Seatwork: Each phonics lesson also has an accompanying student assignment in the *Christ-Centered Phonics Workbook,* which continues to teach to children's spirits while providing them with a solid phonics foundation. (Workbooks are divided into three different levels to allow for differing abilities of four-, five-, and six-year-olds.)

As students proceed through the entire phonics program, which is usually completed by the end of first or second grade, they will have a thorough knowledge of the 44 elementary speech sounds used in American English. They will also acquire spelling, beginning grammar, and writing skills. Because their vocabulary expands rapidly, students just seem to "slide into" multi-syllabled words. By adding a few general syllabication and accent rules, they are well on their way toward proficiency in the second and third levels (comprehension/application) of reading! Reading selections, of course, would be consistent with Philippians 4:8.

Though all of this may seem beyond the comprehension of a little child, it really isn't. Remember, by intuition, children's souls lay hold on many things which their minds may not yet comprehend. The high and ideal thoughts communicated through a godly parent/teacher facilitate and hasten the acquisition and assimilation of subject matter that many might consider too difficult.

Again and again we have found that these little ones grow into the biblical vocabulary used throughout instruction. After all, God has promised that His Word will not return to Him void! It will accomplish the purpose for which He sends it forth (Isa 55:11)! By teaching children's spirits first, God, as the One who teaches us knowledge, opens their intellects.

REVEALING GOD THROUGH MATH

> *"Thou art worthy, O Lord, to receive glory and honour and power: for thou hast created all things, and for thy pleasure they are and were created"* (Rev 4:11).

As Creator of all things, every discipline somehow mirrors His image. Therefore, Christ's image, having been removed through secularization, must be restored to have God-centered, God-purposed education.

Christ is worthy of any effort necessary to do so! As an act of worship, we then have the precious privilege of passing on each sparkling jewel of reflection to His lambs. What a wondrous and high calling to be used by God to feed them in such a manner!

Because math itself reflects God's very nature, His unity yet plurality, this subject is especially exciting to teach. For instance, even counting can teach biblical truths. One of the first things Scripture records God doing is numbering the days of the week. This is also one of the first mathematical skills children learn. As an example of creation, counting the parts of the body is an excellent application of Psalm 139:14: "I will praise You, for I am fearfully and wonderfully made. . . ."

Counting the days of creation and then briefly discussing the biblical numerology of numbers 1-7 can likewise build faith.

Beginning Number Concepts. At RBCS, we teach:

1. **One** is God's number. As Creator, He must be first.

2. **Two** is the number of division. God divided the light from darkness to create two divisions of our day — day and night.

3. **Three** is the number of the Trinity. The triune God was present at creation. The Word, one with the Father, was with Him when the world was made; all things were made by Jesus Christ. The Spirit of God moved upon the face of the waters (Gen 1:2).

4. **Four** is the number of creation. There are four corners of the earth, four seasons, four principal points on the compass, and so forth.

5. **Five** is the number of grace. Grace means unmerited favor, or you might say, "God's riches at Christ's expense." All of God's wonderful creation is a gift of love, not because we deserve it but solely because Jehovah purposed it that way.

6. **Six** is man's number. God created man on the sixth day.

7. **Seven** is the number of spiritual perfection or completion. On the seventh day Jehovah rested; His work was perfect and complete. It was "good."

Our teachers, however, do not present biblical numerology as an absolute. Some doctrines in Scripture are called "absolutes" because the Word of God teaches them so clearly. Salvation by grace alone is an example of this. However, other doctrines should be held more tentatively because godly men may vary in interpretations. Biblical numerology and color typology fit into the latter category. We must deal with the Word honestly. Therefore, we should carefully differentiate between doctrines considered "absolutes" and those upon which honest men allow liberty.

Counting, which involves two basic skills with young children, is an absolute. Rote counting (reciting a sequence of numbers) is the first and easiest skill to acquire. Our Florida sand is ideal for introducing number sequence. A teacher holds up a handful and asks, "Can anyone count how many grains of sand are in my hand, or at the beach? Or, can anyone count the number of stars in the sky? I know Someone who can. God! For He made each and every one! Like Him, the numbers He created are eternal. This means that they go on and on and on. No matter how far we count, there would still be a larger number! What a wonderful Creator!"

Counting by rote is "coat hanger" teaching. Associating the oral count to each object being counted puts meaning to it. This skill takes a little longer to develop. For example, three-year-olds (or even young fours) commonly might look at a bowl containing an apple, orange, and banana and quickly count, "One, two, three, four, five. . . ."

To overcome this tendency, we might say, "Please touch each piece of fruit as you count; say one number for each piece." "Hands on" teaching helps to make math more concrete for preschoolers.

Even little children can perceive that counting "1, 2, 3, 4, and so on" gives recognition that there is plurality, or diversity in God's creation. They can likewise comprehend that His unity is involved in counting "like kinds." For example, they can see that there is no way to relate a tennis shoe, an orange, and a rock to come up with a total count of "three." There is one shoe, one orange, and one rock; but there are not three of a kind.

However, counting an apple, orange, and banana is different. Young children can easily place these into the category of "pieces of fruit." Furthermore, they can understand that God's unity is also seen in the fact that it is always true that "1 apple + 1 orange + 1 banana = 3 pieces of fruit." This is quickly accepted as one of His laws for numbers, which never changes because He never changes (Heb 13:8).

Three areas are important to teach about beginning numbers: number concepts ("how many"), number recognition (the ability to identify numbers accurately), and number recall (the ability to write any number from memory).

To teach number concepts, RBCS teachers use "hands on" manipulatives like Snap Cubes, flannelgraph counting aids, a place value chart, place value sticks, and a balance (to teach the equivalence of simple equations). Other good counting objects are blocks, milk jug lids, checkers, large dominoes, magnetic objects, popsicle sticks, and an abacus. All of these are inexpensive yet do the job quite well. In addition, students count objects drawn on the board, pictured on charts or flashcards, as well as those illustrated in workbook exercises. (During more advanced math instruction, children will learn to use Cuisinaire Rods and Base 10 blocks.)

Number recognition is taught through the *Christ-Centered Math Flashcards,* which contain illustrations of animals and large 1–10 numerals. They also use a 0–20 number line, 1–10 concepts chart, 0–100 number chart, plus flannelgraph and magnetic numbers.

Number recall is practiced through board activities, tracing/writing numbers, and worksheets. This skill is more difficult than the other two and is therefore the last to be mastered.

Beginning workbook exercises provide practice on all three: number concepts, number recognition, and number recall. At RBCS, we teach about creation as children learn numbers 1–10.

For example, at the top of one of their exercises teaching number recognition is this verse:

> *"And God said, Let there be a firmament in the midst of the waters, and let it divide the waters from*

the waters. And God called the firmament Heaven"
(Gen 1:6, 8).

After reading the verse, the teacher explains:

"Two is the number of division. God divided the waters into two parts. The firmament speaks of the arch of the sky which we see. On the first day of creation, God divided the light from the darkness into day and night. In the picture lines . . . , count the days of creation, the types of waters, the division of light from darkness. Then circle the number in each box to the right which tells 'how many.'"

Not until RBCS had been in existence five or six years did we begin to realize that math workbooks being used up until that time were subtly teaching a consumerism or "please-me" mentality. Visualized objects were things like ice cream cones, cookies, lollipops, marbles, bicycles, baseballs, footballs, dolls, teddy bears, and other miscellaneous toys.

The problem enters through concentrated doses which not only permeate math texts but also the rest of the materials designed for educating little children. In reality, this is a religious issue.

All curriculum is inherently religious, because a value system, or way of looking at things, is being transmitted. Since children's appetites are naturally bent toward please-me-ism, it is unwise to add fuel to the fire.

Addition/Subtraction. After our students have a good grasp of numbers 1-10, we then put meaning to the advanced drilling of the addition facts. By this point, students have already been drilling the +0s through the +4s. They are just starting drill on the -0s.

Addition is introduced through stories which provide additional information for the now-familiar 1-10 animal math flashcards. These stories were adapted from the Institute in Basic Life Principles' *Character Sketches*, Volumes I and II (with gracious permission by Mr. Bill Gothard).

For example, to introduce the first card and the concept of +0, the teacher holds up the ONE Penguin card and says:

"Scripture teaches that we can learn more about our triune God by carefully observing His creation (Rom 1:20). Therefore we can see our great God's wisdom even by studying the lives of animals, such as those represented on our 1-10 math cards. Today, we're going to learn about the whole ONE Penguin family — the father and mother penguin and their chick, whom we'll call 1+0. **(She shows the small 1+0 card.)** For our lesson today, let us travel in our imaginations far, far, away to the cold Antarctic — a land of much snow and ice. The Antarctic is the special home God created which is 'just right' for penguin families.

"We can see one of God's most precious qualities — generosity — through observing the lives of father penguins especially. God has created them to be willing to put aside their own wishes to meet the needs of another. For example, when it came time for Mother Penguin to give birth to 1+0, she laid the chick egg, then left, because God gave her the job of going out to sea to find food. While she was away for 3 1/2 months, Mr. ONE Penguin protected little 1+0 from the severe cold by cradling the egg carefully on his warm feet. Not only did the father penguin give up eating during this time, but he barely moved lest the egg roll away and break open too soon. It is only through such sacrificial giving of the father penguins that 1+0, and other chicks like him, are able to receive new life. We can apply this example of generosity to our own lives by asking God to give us also a heart which wants to give sacrificially for the benefit of others!"

She continues with the mathematical language to introduce the "plus 0" facts through 10, which goes something like this. The teacher holds up the small penguin flashcard 1+0 and asks:

> "How many babies do Mr. and Mrs. ONE Penguin have? (Ans: They have one baby.) If there is one baby in my hand, and Mr. and Mrs. ONE Penguin have no more, then 1 plus 0 equals 1. The baby's last name is 1, just the same as his parents'. His first name is 1, his middle name is 0, and his last name is 1."

Next, she shows the animal babies 2+0 through 10+0. She points out that they all have the same middle name, "plus 0," but different first and last names. Then she asks, "Does anyone notice something special about the 'plus 0s' first and last names?" (Ans: In each family, the first and last name is the same. In the TWO family, the first and last name is 2; in the THREE family, the first and last name is 3, and so forth.)

Even though the "plus 0s" are sequentially first, we begin to teach the concept of addition with the "plus 1s" because "adding 1" is concrete; "adding 0" is abstract. Addition is presented in as many ways possible because every child learns differently. What may click for one may not for another.

A general principle is to always move from the concrete ("hands on") to the abstract (fact itself). For example, the 1+1 fact is demonstrated by holding one pencil in the left hand and one in the right and asking, "How many pencils are in my left hand? How many would I have if I brought the pencils together? Let's count them. One, two. I have two pencils altogether."

The example is repeated with a variety of objects until the absoluteness of 1+1=2 is grasped. Then she continues, "When God created numbers, He created laws to govern His creation. Isn't it wonderful that we can therefore know that 1+1 is always equal to 2 without having to count it every time?" This helps establish the reason for learning (memorizing) the laws which govern mathematics.

As a practical application on the "plus 0" lesson, the teacher reads, "The Lord our God is one Lord . . ." (Mark 12:29). She continues with these worksheet instructions:

> "'One Lord' means that there is not another. The picture of the 1 Penguin baby shows 1 penguin and no other. This can be stated as: 1+0=1. The pictures . . . represent a number of objects plus 'no other.' Count the pictures, then write the number in the little square underneath to show 'how many.' Finally, write the number for the total number of pictures counted (the sum) in the last little square."

Instruction is continued over a period of months on "plus ones" through "plus fours" and the reversals (for instance, 4+1/1+4, 3+2/2+3, 6+4/4+6). This procedure also teaches number sequences, as does learning the number families. As an example, the "six" number family is as follows:

$$\begin{array}{ccccccc} 6 & 5 & 4 & 3 & 2 & 1 & 0 \\ +0 & +1 & +2 & +3 & +4 & +5 & +6 \end{array}$$

Subtraction is taught according to a similar procedure (introducing the "minus zeros," "minus ones," and so on), but in reverse. Children learn that addition/subtraction is a doing/undoing relationship.

Word Problems. Solving word problems while learning addition/subtraction provides lessons on how God intends numbers to be used practically. However, since the content of word problems can clearly communicate a value system, selections should be made carefully.

"The magazine clip of a rifle can hold eight cartridges. How many cartridges can two clips hold?"

This word problem accompanies illustrations of grenades and machine guns on a Sandinistas' math sheet used to teach revolutionary ethics while developing multiplication skills.

Satan is not as blatant in this country. He knows that parents in a nation founded upon biblical principles would not stand for it. So he has to be far more subtle, here a little, there a little.

"Susie bought two lollipops for 10 cents each. How much did the lollipops cost altogether?"

"Johnny ate one quart of strawberries. How many pints did he eat?"

"Betty bought a jar of bubbles for $1.98. How much change should she receive from $5.00?"

"At the toy store, Bobby saw 42 skate boards. Of that number, 23 were made of wood, and the remainder were made of plastic. How many skate boards were plastic?"

Now contrast those with a typical word problem at the turn of the century.

"Three boys, Peter, George, and Jacob, can do a piece of work in 3 days. Peter can do it alone in 12 days, and Peter and Jacob can do it in 8 days. How long will it take each of them to do it?"

The latter is from an 1892 math text used by my husband's grandmother when she was only 11. Throughout that book and others from the same era, a work ethic permeated word problems. Bit by bit, they instilled a value system. Bit by bit, so do those typical of today. (Praise God, there are Christian publishers who are recognizing and trying to correct this problem.)

As the children are ready for it, word problems are expanded to adding more than two numbers. For example, consider this problem: "John brought 2 apples to share at lunchtime. Sally brought 3 apples. Frank's Mom packed 2 oranges. Jim brought only 1 apple and a toy car in his lunchbox. How many apples could be shared altogether?"

The relevant data applies to apples only, not the oranges or the car. Students must listen very carefully to pick out the key words. This problem can also be varied by asking, "How many pieces of fruit were brought altogether?" They are also asked, "Which item brought for lunchtime does not apply? Why?" (The toy car is not a food item.) Problems like this can be very exciting as we watch these little ones develop character as well as thinking skills!

Place Value. The teaching of place value is another example of the privilege of sharing a sparkling jewel which reflects our precious Lord! Consider how the beauty of biblical truths can be combined with introducing fives to place value. (By this time, "coat hanger" teaching has already been taught for one semester using a place value pocket chart and popsicle sticks.)

"The LORD our God is one LORD. . . . And his name one," explains the teacher (Deut 6:4, Zech 14:9). She continues, "There is 'not another' God besides Jehovah; Jesus is one Lord! His name is one! Because one is God's number, one is very important throughout Scripture. One is also very important in math because one is the unit by which we count objects in God's creation. To fully exercise dominion over His earth, we must be able to count objects and record 'how many.' The picture [I'm holding] represents the Shekinah glory cloud, a manifestation of our one God's glory over the tabernacle — one dwelling place for Jehovah."

Next, she says, "God said, 'Speak unto the children of Israel. . . . And let them make me a sanctuary; that I may dwell among them' (Ex 25:2, 8).

"God had visited, even walked and talked with such men as Enoch, Noah, and Abraham, but prior to the tabernacle, there had never been a time in which God actually dwelt among men. The tabernacle was God's sanctuary, or holy dwelling place. There, sacrifices were offered repeatedly for sin — a picture of God's Son, our Savior, Who would some day offer one sacrifice for sins forever. Just as the tabernacle was a dwelling place for manifesting the glory of God, so the ones place is the dwelling place for ones. The ones place will hold up to 9 ones."

Examples are demonstrated using a place value pocket chart and popsicle sticks. The children then complete their worksheet by counting the ones and recording them in the ones house, or place.

Now the teacher reads, "And he [Moses] wrote upon the tables the words of the covenant, the ten commandments" (Ex 34:28).

"Ten is the number of completeness of divine order. The covenant between God and Israel established on Mount Sinai incorporated the ten commandments. These commandments were divinely complete because they summarized Israel's responsibility to Jehovah and to each other. The 2 (number of division) tablets represent a division between commands concerning God and commands concerning each other."

The teacher holds a picture of the two tablets while she speaks. Underneath the one which contains the first four commands is written "Responsibility to Jehovah." Underneath the second, containing commandments five through ten, is written "Responsibility to Each Other." She and the class read the complete group of ten commandments, then discuss the application of each.

The introduction to place value continues with reading some of God's instructions for building the tabernacle which contain references to ten.

She then points out, "Remember, 10 is the number of completeness of divine order. The verses [I just read] list a few of God's instructions to Moses for the building of the tabernacle — an earthly dwelling place of Jehovah's glory. Notice the repeat of groups of 10 in the verses.

"Because God created numbers with a purpose, 10 is very important in math. Ten is the 'grouping together' number that enables us to count to very large numbers. We have said that the one's place only holds 9 ones. 10 ones must be grouped together to become 1 group of 10. Tens have a special place also, just like the tabernacle was a special place for Jehovah's glory to be manifested. The tens place is always the next place to the left of the one's place. The ten's place will hold, or record, only 9 tens."

After further demonstration, students apply that knowledge by counting the tens and ones and recording them in the appropriate places, or houses. Whenever there is a 0 in the left hand place, or house, it is written as an invisible zero. Next, the teacher reads, "According to all that the LORD commanded him, so did he. So Moses finished the work. Then a cloud covered the tent of the congregation, and the glory of the LORD filled the tabernacle" (Ex 40:16, 33-34).

She explains, "Moses did all that Jehovah commanded him. In complete submission, Moses chose the Lord's way instead of his own. When the work of building the tabernacle, God's holy dwelling place, was completed, Almighty God was pleased to come dwell among men. Today, the dwelling place of Jehovah is within each individual believer. Our bodies are the temples of the Holy Spirit. And, like Moses, we must be in complete submission to Jehovah — the Lord Jesus Christ. Just as the tabernacle was, and believers are, a dwelling place of God, so the one's and ten's places are dwelling places for ones and tens."

In each problem on their worksheet, children then count the number of tens and ones in the picture and tell "how many" in the appropriate houses, or places. The first one is done for them as an example.

Instruction continues for a month or so on place value, greater than/less than comparisons and two- and three-digit addition/subtraction. After that, students begin instruction on fractions, time, and money. They learn that God wants all of us, not just a fraction of our lives, as they work on examples that begin with Scripture. Contrary to common practice, instruction on telling time does not begin with a clock face. We begin with God's creation of time, different ways of telling time down through the centuries, then a challenge to learn to tell time so they can make better use of it for the Lord. Rather than starting off with simply an identification of coins, students learn about the bartering system in the days of Abraham, how God hates dishonesty in finances, and that we should learn about money so that we can be wise stewards of what God has given us. Math instruction concludes with learning the difficult addition/subtraction teen combinations. By this time, students have had a strong foundation in math so that they can more quickly understand the base 10 system.

Math Ideas for the Home. In the home, there are many opportunities to make math practical in the natural course of every day living. This is by far the best environment to show how everything God created has its little mathematical tab.

Here are some simple ideas. At a mealtime, ask your child to "serve" the family by counting how many will be eating, then setting out the correct number of napkins, knives, forks, spoons, glasses, and plates.

Should 6 forks be needed but only 4 are counted, ask, "How many more do you need to make 6 altogether? How can that be stated as one of God's laws for numbers?" (Ans: "4 + 2 = 6.") Actually writing the equation would enrich the teaching moment.

Or, suppose your child counts out 6 and needs only 4, then ask, "How many should you take away? How can that be stated as one of God's laws for numbers?" (Ans: "6 - 2 = 4.")

A little girl might enjoy combining "stewardship" of her hair with counting brush strokes (25, 50, or even 100 times). A boy can do the same with brushing his teeth.

To encourage speedier completion of a task, see if your child can "beat you" before you count to 5 or 10 slowly. (At RBCS, as long as we know a student is earnestly trying to do so, we adjust the speed of the count so he "wins.")

While you are busy on another task, have your child string # beads, stack # blocks, or clap # times. When finished, he could write the number which tells "how many" on a chalkboard or paper. Or, a young child could visibly identify the number representing "how many" by using a flannelgraph or magnetic number.

When your child is likely to be underfoot, why not suggest he count out the number of magnetic objects you name and then slide the magnetic number which tells "how many" beside the total objects counted.

Even getting dressed in the morning can be a teaching moment. While doing so, have your child button # buttons on a blouse or shirt. Ask, "How many more buttons are left to be buttoned if we leave the top one open?" or "How many buttons are there altogether?"

Matching socks is a good technique. This teaches pairs plus the identification of patterns and colors. Another good method is to count illustrated objects in a book during storytime.

The practicality of knowing number sequence can be reinforced by marking off a calendar each day until a special event. (Count how many days have been marked off plus how many days are left until the event.) Using a growth chart to record increasing height also teaches number sequence, as does provision of a ruler or yardstick to measure things. Boys showing their love by "helping" Daddy with carpentry is an excellent opportunity to teach measuring. Or girls "helping" Mommy sew.

The concept of fractions can be taught by helping your child identify one dozen eggs and 1/2 dozen eggs (hardboiled works best!). Or, start with anything whole, such as a sandwich, pie, orange, pizza, or cake. Divide that whole into 2 parts; discuss that 1 part of 2 is called 1/2. Divide into 4 parts; 1 part of 4 is called 1/4. (Do this with other fractions as well.)

An excellent means to show the importance of numbers is in preparation of recipes ("how many" for different ingredients, liquid measures, dry measures, fractions, temperature).

Helping to prepare a meal also teaches responsibility. Daughters, especially, should be trained in household arts from an early age.

Giving a child plastic measuring cups and spoons to play "house" or for use in the sandbox is another suggestion. Plastic gallon, half gallon, quart, and pint containers can teach a lot about liquid measuring and can be a welcome "treat" on a hot summer day by getting to fill them from a water hose outside!

Teaching "time" involves both number sequence and fractions. On a large-faced clock, have your child count by 5s or 10s to 60 minutes on an hour, to 30 on a half hour, or 15 for a quarter hour. Establishing time limits for accomplishing a task, followed by a time period for play, is a good way to teach the stewardship concept.

For a dawdler at the table, using a 15-minute timer to visualize a time limit for completion of a meal is beneficial. However, be sure to forewarn of a suitable consequence if not finished in that time period. (This worked well in our own family!)

Before/after concepts can be taught while shopping to "show love to Daddy by finding bargains." Ask your child to hand you the item which is before (or after) the one you name. (Reading skills can be developed by this method, too.) In the home, before/after can be reinforced by using terms like, "Your turn is after Susie's but before Johnny's." Or, you might say, "Before 12:00 you may play; after 12:00 we will be eating lunch."

Number identification can be reinforced through an example like this. If buying soup, and two "like kinds" have the prices of 43 cents and 39 cents, ask your child to hand you the one you specify. To develop greater than/less than skills, have him do the comparison pricing on like items to find the "greater" or "lesser" price. He should first identify the prices for you and then indicate the lesser (or greater) priced one, selecting one from the shelf upon your approval.

On non-routine tasks, you might pay a little wage. After completing the agreement, teach him to give to the Lord first, then plan wise usage of the funds to stretch his dollars. This could be simply done by paying his wages in a manner which facilitates placing the Lord's in one container, savings in another, and spending money in a third.

Doing "odd jobs" to earn a watch is a suggestion. He could then learn to personally refer to "his watch" for the proper time to get up, go to bed, have lunch, schooling, and so forth. This also develops responsibility and punctuality.

Perhaps your child could even do special little jobs for a next door neighbor, or grandparents. (However, make sure children understand that they should not be paid for everything they do.) Preparation for such a job opportunity could be done in the form of a word problem. Use word problems which are practical to your child's life.

Math becomes even more practical as your child learns the actual cost of personal things, like a pencil, eraser, paper, ball, crayons, coloring book, barrettes, ribbons, or hair brush.

One way is to have your child count out correct amounts for small purchases at the store. At age five, our Lynda was able to figure the total cost for crayons and a coloring book plus how much change she should receive out of $1.00. (She also carefully watched the cashier to ensure that correct change was given!)

These are just a few examples of all the great opportunities for teaching math in the home — here a little and there a little! I am sure you can think of many more! The point is to make yourself conscious of everyday teaching moments which would otherwise slip away, wasting the precious time God has given with His heritage.

Chapter Ten

"Who, Me, LORD?"

"When you said, 'Seek My face,' my heart said to You, 'Your face, Lord, I will seek'" (Psa 27:8).

Years ago, I used to envision writing a book entitled *From Beneath a Rock*. On the cover was a caricature of a huge boulder with only my face peering out from underneath, looking toward heaven as I feebly questioned, "Who, me, Lord?"

That book was to praise God for victory over the days when my normal response to His challenges was scurrying back under "my rock" to hide. Through the living and written Word, however, He slowly plied me from beneath "my rock" and caused me to stand *on* the Rock, Jesus Christ!

I am neither a "Super Wife," "Super Mom," nor "Super Teacher." One thing, and one thing only, changed my life — as it can yours! When He said, "Seek My face," my heart said to Him, "Your face, Lord, I will seek!"

Beloved, God uses ordinary people like us (and our children) to advance His kingdom on earth (1 Cor 1:26-29)!

All it takes is an obedient and teachable heart. God's child is a living sacrifice who wants to live in worshiping submission to Him, a person who wants every thought, word, and deed to be an act of worship, demonstrating His indescribable worth. The Lord then works out in us whatever is necessary to fulfill His calling and live for His glory (Phil 2:13). In turn, we are to train His heritage to do the same.

THE CHALLENGE

It is no "accident" that this book has come into your hands. The Lord has a purpose for its doing so. Your responsibility is to prayerfully seek that purpose, then carry out whatever He lays on your heart.

If you sense that He is calling you to formally teach your little ones, at least for their formative years, feelings of inadequacy may prompt your own, "Who, me, Lord?"

Beloved, feelings of inadequacy can be a blessing in disguise. What counts is not *what* you know but *Whom* you know!

It is not our ability that He is after, but availability. As an encouragement to you, let me share something from a true incident in 1984.

"When did you get your doctorate?" quizzed Gloria Parkhurst. She had just arrived in Niceville to attend a week-long seminar I was conducting on Christ-Centered Early Childhood Education. At that time, Gloria was herself working on a doctorate. Since teachers were traveling from various states to attend, she assumed that I must have a long list of the world's credentials to warrant doing so.

"I don't have a doctorate, Gloria," came the reply, with a smile.

"Well, surely you're close to getting one, aren't you?"

Wondering if she would take the next transportation out of town after hearing my answer, I honestly informed, "Gloria, I only have a high school diploma. What you are about to receive during this week is a result of earnestly seeking the Lord's face to find His answers for early childhood."

She not only stayed but also joined the RBCS kindergarten team a few months later. Gloria and I became good friends.

The point is that having no special formal training forced me to rely on God's strength, not my own.

Again and again I found God to be faithful, willing to meet my every need. Even when the flesh cried out to Him, and to RBCS Superintendent Bob Grete, "But I'm unqualified!" the response from both was always the same: "Persevere in doing good, Doreen!" So I now pass that same life-changing exhortation on to you, dear sister. Persevere in doing good!

We are Sarah's "daughters" if we do (1 Pet 3:1-6)! She too struggled with "Who, me, Lord?" God's response? "Is anything too hard for the LORD?" (Gen 18:14). Through Christ, you can be submissive to your husband as to the Lord. Through Christ, you can be an example of faith in word and in deed to your children. Through Christ, you can teach them formally. Stand on the Rock as your strength (Phil 4:13)! For He will never leave nor forsake you (Heb 13:5)!

Fight the good fight of faith! Seek knowledge. Gain a firm hold on why home schooling itself is such a precious calling. Attending a "Home Schooling Workshop" by Gregg Harris, Director of Christian Life Workshops, is an excellent means to give you and your husband such a foundation. It is also a great way to meet other home schooling families and learn of support groups which can help encourage folk like yourself.

If you are unable to attend a seminar in person, cassettes of the workshop are available for purchase. A seminar schedule and listing of tapes can be obtained by writing Christian Life Workshops (P.O. Box 2250, Gresham, OR 97030). Or, call (800)225-5259. In addition, you may wish to read Gregg Harris's book *The Christian Home School* (Brentwood, TN: Wolgemuth and Hyatt Publishers, 1988).

My "A WOMAN TO BE PRAISED" seminar might also be of interest. This seminar combines additional information on how to love your husband and children biblically, plus "how to's" on teaching phonics, reading, and math. If I can be of service to you and your friends, feel free to contact me at (800)884-7858 for a schedule or information on how to sponsor one in your own town.

Subscribing to a good home schooling magazine, such as *The Teaching Home* (Box 20219, Portland, OR 97220, Phone: (503)253-9633) can be very helpful. This magazine contains articles on home schooling which are both practical and inspirational. The latest legal issues concerning home schooling are regularly presented. Advertisements for curriculum materials can also be found, including an ad by Christ Centered Publications (CCP).

CCP prints and markets the "Christ-Centered Curriculum for Early Childhood" program, portions of which were presented in this book. CCP is located on the Rocky Bayou Christian School campus (2101 N. Partin Drive, Niceville, FL 32578, (800) 884-7858).

Originally, producing a curriculum for use by other Christian schools and home schooling parents was not in RBCS plans at all. Being unable to find early childhood curricula which we believed truly took every moment captive for Christ, we felt led to develop a few materials for our own use. However, God surprised us when He revealed that He had a broader ministry in mind. While the curriculum was still in its early stages, word began to get out about what we were doing.

Letters started arriving, asking if we were willing to share with others. What started off as a few items to enrich our kindergarten program turned out to be a decade-long project. The final outcome was a full phonics, reading, and math program for three-year-olds through first graders.

232

RBCS owns the copyright on the Christ-centered materials. Income above CCP's operating expenses goes back to the school to strengthen its ministry to students and their families, as well as numerous home schoolers under the "umbrella" of RBCS.

Beloved, the motivation for writing this book was not to "sell" curriculum. Rather, in obedience, I felt compelled to share the message God burned into my heart during its development. But it would be a disservice to you if I didn't at least mention that there is curriculum available which implements that message. And, I must be honest, it would bring great joy to my heart if God leads some of you to take advantage of that labor of love!

Should your husband not grant permission to home school or there is some other valid reason for your not teaching your little one personally, then I exhort you to prayerfully look into a Christian school education. However, be careful. Having the name "Christian" does not necessarily make it so. Like a good Berean, you should investigate any school thoroughly before entrusting your child to its care.

It is wise to invest time observing classes to evaluate the atmosphere and curriculum content. (RBCS has an "open house" observation policy; most schools do as well.) Remember, your child's teacher is the one who will be standing at "the window" of his heart. Therefore, it is important to find out what type of discipleship example will be set. Suppose a school is committed to doing things God's way but the curriculum content is weak. Perhaps sharing this book with the principal and kindergarten teacher may be welcomed. Or, supplement educationally at home through extra teaching from a biblical perspective. As your children move on into the elementary grades and beyond, Ruth Haycock's four volume set *Bible Truths for School Subjects* (available through Christian Life Workshops) can further enrich your understanding of the biblical perspective of subjects. Regardless of their ages, never lose sight of the fact that "children are a heritage from the LORD, the fruit of the womb is a reward. Like arrows in the hand of a warrior, so are the children of one's youth. Happy is the man who has his quiver full of them . . ." (Psa 127:3–5).

Like warriors, we are to one day aim those "rewards" as straight arrows into the battle so that they hit their designated targets! This means that they will have been discipled to hold the biblical world view and possess the godly character and academic skills necessary to fulfill God's calling and live for His glory. This all begins in their formative years, here a little and there a little, ever sharpening the tips of those arrows by the precious Sword of the Spirit!

THE GREAT REWARD

Making disciples in that manner may well produce the fruit of a giant like George Mueller, an Englishman known for his unique walk of faith. When asked his secret of service, he replied:

> *"There was a day when I died, utterly died to George Mueller," and, as he spoke, he bent lower and lower until he almost touched the floor — "to his opinions, preferences, tastes, and will; died to the world, its approval or censure; died to the approval or blame of even my brethren and friends. Since then I have studied to show myself approved only unto God."*

May God Himself likewise become our reward — and our children's — not joy, nor peace, nor even blessing, but God Himself! "Oh, the depth of the riches both of the wisdom and knowledge of God! How unsearchable are His judgments and His ways past finding out! For who has known the mind of the LORD? Or who has become His counselor? Or who has first given to Him and it shall be repaid to him? For of Him and through Him and to Him are all things, to whom be glory forever. Amen" (Rom 11:33-36). And Amen!

To become Christ's living sacrifices and then disciple our children to do the same, what higher or more precious calling could we have? Is He not worth any price? Are not our children? Mom, through Christ, what a difference *you* can make!

❧ ENDNOTES ❧

1. A.W. Tozer, *The Knowledge of the Holy.* ©1961 by A.W. Tozer. All rights reserved. Published by Harper & Row Publishers, San Francisco, California. Used by permission.

2. J. Hudson Taylor, *Union and Communion.* © by J. Hudson Taylor. All rights reserved. Published by Bethany House Publishers, Minneapolis, Minnesota. Used by permission.

3. Mrs. Charles E. Cowman, *Streams in the Desert.* ©1950 by Mrs. Charles E. Cowman. All rights reserved. Published by Cowman Publications, Inc., Los Angeles, California. Used by permission.

4. Jack and Carole Mayhall, *Marriage Takes More Than Love.* ©1978 by Jack and Carole Mayhall. All rights reserved. Published by Navpress, Colorado Springs, Colorado. Used by permission.

5. Kenneth O. Gangel, *Toward a Biblical Theology of Marriage and Family,* published in the Journal of Psychology and Theology, Winter 1977 edition. ©1977 by Kenneth O. Gangel. All rights reserved. Used by permission.

6. Frank E. Gaebelein, Christian Education, *The New International Dictionary of the Christian Church.* ©1974 by Frank E. Gaebelein. All rights reserved. Published by The Zondervan Corporation. Used by permission.

7. Maynard Hatcher, *That Pesky Needle's Eye*, published in the Presbyterian Journal. ©1984 by Maynard Hatcher. All rights reserved. Used by permission.

8. A. Cohen, *Everyman's Talmud.* ©1949 by A. Cohen. All rights reserved. Published by E. P. Dutton Co., New York. Used by permission.

9. Alice Morse Earle, *Child Life in Colonial Days.* ©1899 by Alice Morse Earle. All rights reserved. Published by The MacMillan Co. Used by permission.

10. Neil Postman, *Amusing Ourselves to Death*. ©1985 by Neil Postman. All rights reserved. Published by Penguin Books, New York. Used by permission.

11. William B. Sprague, *Annals of the American Pulpit,* Vol. I. ©1985 by William B. Sprague. All rights reserved. Published by Arnos Press & *The New York Times*, New York. Used by permission.

12. David Elkind, *The Hurried Child*. ©1981 by David Elkind. All rights reserved. Published by Addison-Wesley Publishing Company, New York. Used by permission.

13. Kenneth O. Gangel and Warren S. Benson, *Christian Education: Its History and Philosophy*. ©1983 by Kenneth O. Gangel and Warren S. Benson. All rights reserved. Published by Moody Press, Chicago, Illinois. Used by permission.

14. Colleen Dedrick, *Unschooling: The Ungodly Education*, published in *Circumspectus*, No. 12, Summer 1984. All rights reserved. Used by permission.

15. Samuel Blumenfeld, *Who Killed Excellence?* ©1985 by Samuel Blumenfeld. All rights reserved. Published in *Imprimis* magazine, Vol. 14, No. 9. Used by permission.

16. Rudolf Flesch, *Why Johnny Can't Read—And What You Can Do About It*. ©1955 by Rudolf Flesch. All rights reserved. Published by Harper & Row, New York. Used by permission.

17. Os Guinness, *The Gravedigger File*. ©1983 by Os Guinness. All rights reserved. Published by Inter-Varsity Press, Downers Grove, Illinois. Used by permission.

18. Allan Bloom, *The Closing of the American Mind*. ©1983 by Alan Bloom. All rights reserved. Published by Simon & Schuster, New York. Used by permission.

19. John A. Stormer, *Growing Up God's Way*. ©1983 by John A. Stormer. All rights reserved. Published by Liberty Bell Press, Florissant, Missouri. Used by permission.

20. Rudolf Flesch, *Why Johnny Still Can't Read*. ©1981 by Rudolf Flesch. All rights reserved. Published by Harper & Row, New York. Used by permission.

21. Jeanne S. Chall, *Learning to Read: The Great Debate.* ©1981 by Jeanne S. Chall. All rights reserved. Published by McGraw-Hill, New York. Used by permission.

22. Allan C. Brownfield, *Why Are Our Schools Producing Illiterates?* ©1981 by Allan C. Brownfield. All rights reserved. Published in *Human Events,* August 17, 1985. Used by permission.

23. Phyllis Schlafly, *The Phyllis Schlafly Report,* Vol. 22, No. 1, August 1988. ©1988 by Phyllis Schlafly. All rights reserved. Used by permission.

24. James L. Hymes, *Teaching Reading to the Under Six age: A Child Development Point of View.* ©1970 by James L. Hymes. All rights reserved. Used by permission.

25. Paul W. Jehle, *Go Ye Therefore and Teach.* ©1982 by Paul W. Jehle. All rights reserved. Published by Plymouth Rock Foundation, Plymouth, Massachusetts, and Marlborough, New Hampshire. Used by permission.

26. Rose Weiner, *Friends of God.* ©1983 by Rose Weiner. All rights reserved. Published by Maranatha Publications, Gainesville, Florida. Used by permission.

27. *The Christian World View of Science and Technology.* ©1986 by The Coalition of Revival, Inc. All rights reserved. Published by the Coalition of Revival, Inc., Mountain View, California. Used by permission.

28. Francis A. Schaeffer, *Art and the Bible.* ©1973 by Francis A. Schaeffer. All rights reserved. Published by Inter-Varsity Press, Downers Grove, Illinois. Used by permission.

29. Leonard J. Seidel, *God's New Song: A Biblical Perspective of Music.* ©1973 by Leonard J. Seidel. All rights reserved. Published by Grace Unlimited Publications, Springfield, Virginia. Used by permission.

30. Gary and Anne Marie Ezzo, *Preparation for Parenting.* ©1986 by Gary and Anne Marie Ezzo. All rights reserved. Published by Grace Community Church, Sun Valley, California. Used by permission.

31. J. Richard Fugate, *What the Bible Says . . . About Child Training.* ©1980 by J. Richard Fugate. All rights reserved. Published by Aletheia Publishers, Tempe, Arizona. Used by permission.

32. Jack Fennema, *Nurturing Children in the Lord.* ©1977 by Jack Fennema. All rights reserved. Published by Presbyterian and Reformed Publishing Co., Phillipsburg, New Jersey. Used by permission.

33. Robert McCurry, *Parents and the Education of Their Children.* ©1985 by Robert McCurry. All rights reserved. Published by Temple Press, East Point, Georgia. Used by permission.

34. Phil Phillips, *Turmoil in the Toybox.* ©1986 by Phil Phillips. All rights reserved. Published by Starburst Publishers, Lancaster, Pennsylvania. Used by permission.

35. T. Van Der Kooy, "Distinctive Features of the Christian School." ©1977 by T. Van Der Kooy. All rights reserved. Published in *The Journal of Christian Reconstruction,* Vol. IV, Summer 1977, Vallecito, California. Used by permission.

36. Dr. Laurence J. Peter, *Peter's Quotations: Ideas For Our Time.* ©1977 by Dr. Laurence J. Peter. All rights reserved. Published by Bantam Books, New York. Used by permission.

37. Gregg Harris, "Delight Directed Study." ©1988 by Gregg Harris. All rights reserved. Published in *The Teaching Home,* Feb./Mar. 1988. Used by permission.